BREASTFEEDING
YOUR BABY

BREASTFEEDING YOUR BABY

Revised Edition

SHEILA KITZINGER

Photography by Nancy Durrell McKenna
Breastfeeding Adviser: Chloe Fisher

Alfred A. Knopf   New York 1998

The author

Senior Art Editor Cathy Shilling
Project Editor Caroline Greene
Editor Fergus Collins

Managing Editor Jemima Dunne
Managing Art Editor Lynne Browne

U.S. Editor Leyla Aker

A Dorling Kindersley Book

THIS IS A BORZOI BOOK PUBLISHED BY ALFRED A. KNOPF, INC.

Library of Congress Cataloging in Publication Data

Kitzinger, Sheila.
Breastfeeding your baby / Sheila Kitzinger. — Rev.ed.
    p. cm.
    Includes bibliographical references and index.
    ISBN 0–375–70195–8 (alk.paper)
    1. Breast feeding—Popular works. 1. Title.
RJ216.K58 1998
649'.33—dc21

Published September 11, 1989. This revised and expanded American edition publication September, 1998.

Reproduced by Colourscan (Singapore)

Printed and bound by Garzanti Verga (Italy)

CONTENTS

INTRODUCTION

BREASTFEEDING YOUR BABY is a way of intimately communicating with another human being. It is never just a matter of technique or of filling a baby's stomach with milk as you might fill the tank of the car with gas.

It is true that there are important techniques, the most vital of which is that of helping the baby to get latched on well to the breast. But, because breastfeeding is also an expression of loving, it is connected with your emotions. Techniques cannot be isolated from how you feel about your baby and your body.

LEARNING FROM THE BABY

It is sometimes said that women who read books about breastfeeding are the ones who do not succeed. It is true that a woman's determination may lead to her being so anxious that nothing seems to go right. But many of the skills of breastfeeding come not so much from instinct as from learning. This is learning from the baby—understanding the baby's signals, and responding to them in turn. A baby is a living, sensitive being who is learning and developing; and sending out messages from the moment of birth.

When you see smiling babies in books and films, you may feel that your baby should be like that too and that if she is not, you are not a good enough mother. The truth is that there are very few babies who are in this state of Nirvana all the time. If you believe that your baby must never cry, and that it is a sign of your failure as a woman and a mother if your child does cry, you will feel threatened every time she asserts herself as an independent being.

HAVING CONFIDENCE IN YOURSELF

Breastfeeding is a psychosexual process. I do not mean by this that it produces genital sensations or that it is sexually exploitative. In the United States a few years ago, a four-year-old girl was taken away from her mother by doctors, psychologists and social workers because she

had been in "mouth-breast contact." The idea that to breastfeed is an erotic indulgence or an exercise in power over a child is a perverted view of the breastfeeding relationship. Happy breastfeeding, whether with a baby, a toddler, or an older child who has a specially close "going to bed" time, which includes breastfeeding, can be deeply satisfying for you both. Like other psychosexual experiences, it needs to be based on confidence and a sense of self-worth. Women often lack confidence. When anything goes wrong, we think that it must be our fault. When I was researching my book *Woman's Experience of Sex*,* I talked to women who had been subjected to sexual attack and who had been raped. They always asked themselves, "What did I do wrong?" Lack of confidence is endemic among women—particularly in Western societies, and perhaps the world over.

On the other hand, the questions that so many Western women ask, such as, "Will I be able to breastfeed?" or "Will I try to breastfeed?" are rather like asking, "Can I breathe?" or "Can I walk?" Women in peasant societies do not talk about trying to breastfeed—they know they can do it. This became clear to me when I was doing anthropological field-work in the Caribbean. Jamaican women, who were often inadequately fed and who lived in poverty, accepted that they could feed their babies—and they all did. In Western societies, however, breastfeeding has become a self-conscious activity. A woman feels the same anxiety as she might when facing an important examination.

Yet the free and generous flow of milk does not come from mental concentration. It comes instead from something that I can best describe in a French phrase, which translated means "being happy in your own skin."

In these pages I want to help you acquire the technical skills of breastfeeding, and also help you to develop self-confidence—so that you and your baby can really enjoy breastfeeding.

A GUIDE TO THE NEW EDITION

AN UPSURGE OF RESEARCH into breastfeeding has corroborated what mothers who breastfed happily always knew. I have drawn on this research in these pages. It is a sign of our distrust of the ways we mother that we often turn to experts to justify what we are doing and to give ourselves confidence. On the other hand, it can be useful to quote specific references when talking with critics of breastfeeding. These references are starred (*) in the text (see page 165). For those who only turn to books when they have a particular problem, there is a new chapter on *Solving Problems* (see pages 156–63). Other new pages will help readers who may need medication (see pages 68–71).

WHAT'S NEW?

All mammals feed their young with milk from their own bodies and human mothers have been practicing the skills of breastfeeding for thousands of years. Until the twentieth century a baby who was not breastfed was unlikely to survive. Even now, in countries where babies are fed on formula, while mothers do not have access to a supply of clean water, do not have fridges, and are short of money to buy substitute milk, babies often die before they are a year old. In Brazil, for example, where there is deep concern that formula feeding is responsible for the deaths of 60 percent of babies in shanty towns, great efforts are being made to support breastfeeding.

In Northern industrial countries, even when women are careful about hygiene and how feeds are mixed, their artificially fed babies are more likely to have allergies, tummy upsets, and colds. As adults, they may become diabetic or develop heart disease. Breastfeeding for the first three months protects against gastrointestinal illness even after the baby is no longer breastfed.*

A medical journal put the advantages of breastfeeding this way: "If a new vaccine became available that could prevent one million or more child deaths a year, and that was moreover cheap, safe, and administered orally, and required no cold chain (i.e. need not be kept refrigerated), it would become an immediate health imperative. Breastfeeding could do all this and more."*

Breastfeeding is not just a matter of personal choice, like choosing between brands of breakfast cereal. It is a political issue. How women behave in Northern cultures sets a standard to which others aspire. I once discussed baby feeding with Indian and Pakistani mothers who had emigrated to Northern England, and asked them why they were feeding their babies formula. They answered simply, "We wish to do as your people do." For them, it was the logical consequence of a decision to adapt to a new culture.

Every time a new mother leaves the hospital and is handed a can of dried milk, or when samples and free offers of bottles are included in bounty packs, or every time a health visitor or doctor questions whether a woman is producing enough milk and advises her to give her baby supplements of artificial milk, the chances of a woman breastfeeding are reduced.

Conversely, every time a woman breastfeeds, lets it be known that she is breastfeeding, and is not embarrassed about it, she is defending women's rights everywhere to feed babies with milk from their own bodies.

The human race has survived because women understood how to breastfeed. Good breastfeeding practices are found all over the world. These women may not be able to read or write, but they know how to breastfeed. They may live in poverty but they still know how to breastfeed. We need to find out how they do it.

In my work as a social anthropologist, I have learned that they do not watch clocks and do not limit the number of times the baby suckles. They sleep with their babies and breastfeed generously during the night. They do not offer artificial supplements. They feed freely and casually, without anxiety, letting the milk flow. They are confident that they can breastfeed. So they do.

A CHILD IS BORN

YOUR UTERUS HAS BEEN A SANCTUARY and a nest for your baby for nine long months. You have felt feet kicking, head bouncing, body turning, and knees twisting—all the energetic movements of a baby developing the neuro-muscular coordination and strength to adapt to life in the world outside.

INSIDE THE WOMB

Sucking starts inside the womb. Your baby has been drinking the amniotic fluid in which he has been floating and moving, and even sucking his fingers and thumbs.

He has been stimulated by practice contractions (Braxton-Hicks contractions) of your uterus, by sounds he has heard from both inside and outside your body, by the rocking movement of your pelvis as you walked, and by the sudden rush of hormones in your bloodstream at times when you were highly emotionally aroused.

THE ONSET OF LABOR

Then labor starts. Contractions become firm squeezes and hugs that rise and fall in great waves of action. The hollow muscle in which the baby is contained embraces him so that he curls up into a ball, arms and legs flexed and chin tucked in on his chest. The contractions begin to press him down toward and then through the soft, dilated cervix, and slowly and steadily through the opening accordionlike folds of your vagina.

As he reaches the lowest point in the journey, his face is downward, and the tissues of the posterior wall of the birth canal press against his face and onto his nose and mouth. You push, and he slides forward, edging little by little toward the light and then sinking back as flexible tissues slip over his head again. You push once more.

THE MOMENT OF CROWNING

At last the top of the baby's head reaches the opening and stays there once the contraction has finished. It is the moment of crowning. His head is grasped by your muscles, and you have a tingling, stinging sensation, as if the head were encircled by a ring of fire. The pressure is powerful around the head while you wait for a message from deep inside your body to breathe—and push—and breathe again—and allow your baby's head to inch forward to birth. The head comes slowly and steadily—all the tissues fanning open like the great petals of a rose as your baby surges forward and out. The head dips down under the arch of bone at the front of your pelvis, and then up, releasing the chin. Then the face slides up over your perineum. The amniotic fluid—to which the head has acted as a kind of stopper—now streams out and over the face. The head turns to come into line with the shoulders, which are still inside you. Then the shoulders slide out and the whole body follows, slippery, wet, and warm.

INTO YOUR ARMS

You reach out to draw the baby to you. You hold and enfold this child whom you have only just seen, but who has been part of your body, part of yourself, for 40 weeks or longer, and whose movements have become as familiar to you as the beat of your own heart. This baby is new, but you have been companions on the same journey, and you trust each other. It is one of the most emotional and highly charged moments of your life. However exhausted you feel, from somewhere comes a new surge of energy—as you meet your child for the first time.

The baby turns his head toward your voice, selecting it from every other background sound. He orients himself toward the human voice—above all, to yours. The baby's eyes open and gaze at you steadily.

You feel the firm roundness of the limbs, the silky roundness of the head, and you stroke them in wonder. The newborn is sensitively responsive to touch, and relaxes. The long and difficult journey of labor ends in this safe haven of your welcoming and protective arms.

By the twentieth week of pregnancy a baby is skilled at thumb sucking, practicing coordinated movements that will be needed later for feeding.

WHY BREASTFEED?

Benefits of Breastfeeding

THE BEST WAY TO HELP YOUR BABY grow normally, and to give every possible protection against disease, is to breastfeed for one year, and exclusively for the first five or six months of life.

NUTRITIONAL VALUE OF BREASTMILK

Breastmilk is one of the most energy-dense foods in existence. Its ratio of protein, fat, and carbohydrate concentrations is uniquely adapted to the baby's needs, and varies at different times in the day, even during a single feed. When a baby is put to the breast, the first milk that is available—the foremilk—is watery, so if she is just thirsty, a short suck will satisfy her. The longer a baby sucks from one breast, the more fat and protein she obtains.

It is impossible for artificial milk to adapt to the baby's needs in this way. It is important to continue giving breastmilk after weaning foods have been introduced. A baby would have to eat a huge amount of solid food such as cereal, mashed fruit or vegetables to get the level of nutrition available in breastmilk.

BENEFITS OF LACTOSE

Ninety percent of the carbohydrate in breastmilk is in the form of lactose—milk sugar—compared with 4 percent in cow's milk. In a breastfed baby the passage of milk through the intestines is faster than in a bottle-fed baby. Some of the lactose turns into lactic acid, which has the power to resist harmful bacteria, making the bowel movements looser. Lactose in breastmilk is less sweet than the sucrose added to cow's milk to make infant formula. So bottle-fed babies become used to very sweet milk. Once teeth come through, this can result in tooth decay.

Fat is more easily absorbed from breastmilk than from cow's milk. Babies who do not get enough essential fatty acids develop dermatitis, have a low blood platelet count, which results in

hemorrhages under the skin, are susceptible to infection, and fail to thrive. This combination of symptoms never occurs in breastfed babies.

MINERALS AND VITAMINS

Breastfed babies do not usually require any supplementary minerals or vitamins; in fact, giving supplements unnecessarily can be harmful. A healthy, well-fed woman produces milk rich in all the vitamins and minerals a baby needs. Breastmilk is low in salt, potassium, and chloride; cow's milk has three times as much. Babies do not need this heavy concentration of minerals, and excess quantities harm the kidneys.

Breastmilk also contains the correct balance of calcium, phosphorus, and magnesium, which are important for growth. Breastfed babies are unlikely to be short of iron and zinc. These are also in cow's milk, but are less easily absorbed.

RESISTANCE TO INFECTION

Breastmilk contains at least six anti-infective agents against common childhood illnesses. An artificially fed baby is four times more likely to get pneumonia, and nearly twice as likely to catch a cold. Formula-fed babies are more than twelve times more likely to suffer diarrhea than breastfed babies. Antibodies against viruses and bacteria are present in breastmilk, protecting the respiratory and gastrointestinal tracts.

If there are allergies in your family, your baby will benefit from prolonged breastfeeding. She may still develop asthma or eczema, but the onset is later and less severe. Two percent of babies have an allergy to cow's milk. A baby with this allergy who starts on breastmilk may be able to tolerate some cow's milk after a few months. One final benefit of breastmilk is that it is completely clean. Unless care is taken with sterilizing and making sure the milk is made up fresh, artificial milk may be contaminated.

Breastmilk provides all essential nutrients until the age of one. This older baby is not well latched on, but gets enough milk anyway. A newborn needs to have a good mouthful of breast so as to squeeze milk from the glands.

YOUR BREASTS

Changes in Shape

MANY WOMEN ARE ANXIOUS that breastfeeding will spoil the shape of their breasts. In fact, the major changes occur during pregnancy, and not from breastfeeding. During pregnancy the area around the nipples—the areola—becomes darker, and the little bumps on them (known as Montgomery's tubercles) become more pronounced. In order to make milk, the breasts' glandular tissue increases, and they become fuller and heavier, developing a more generous curve. As a result, the nipples, instead of being centered, are now in the upper part of the breast globes.

These changes make it easier for the baby to feed; he can nestle his chin into the lower part of the breast, get his jaw over the curve of the areola, and clasp the sinuses and glandular tissue firmly with his gums.

Breasts are part of a woman's sexual image in Northern and Western cultures. Sometimes a pregnant woman fears that her male partner may find her fuller, heavier breasts unattractive. It is true that some men prefer small, teenage-shaped breasts, but it is more likely that a loving male partner takes pleasure in a woman's fuller, riper shape. This is the shape breasts need to be for a baby to feed easily.

Perhaps, instead of mourning our lost adolescent breasts, we can take pride in the way our bodies adapt so beautifully.

Your breasts become fuller in pregnancy (inset, opposite). When milk comes in, they swell so that the areola is less prominent and becomes part of the breast's rounded shape (opposite).

The shape of your breasts adapts to the baby's needs in pregnancy. These changes occur early, often within the first eight weeks, and may be the very first thing you notice, even before a thickening waistline.

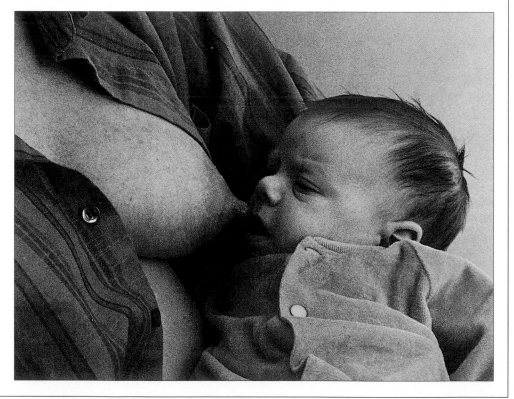

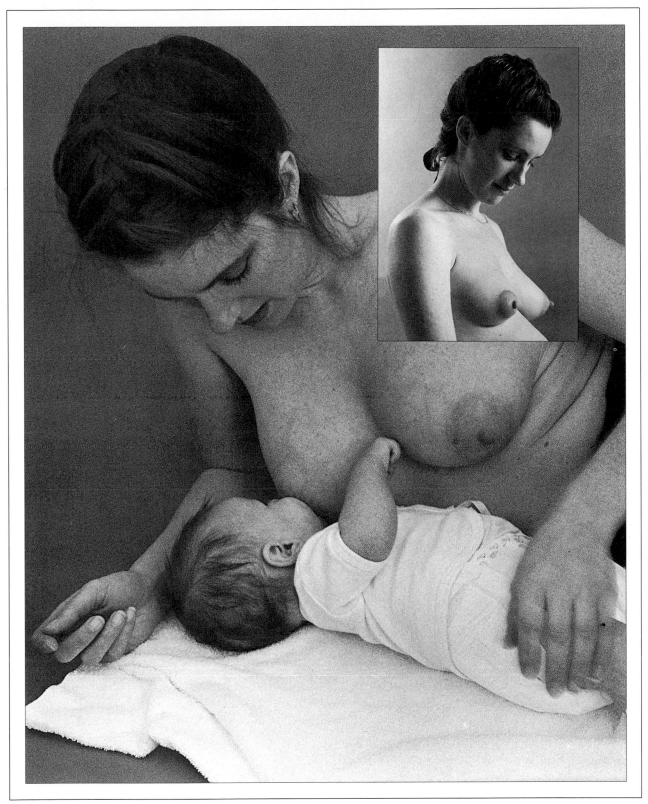

Types of Breast

Your ability to breastfeed successfully does not depend on the size or type of your breasts or nipples—there is no such thing as a perfectly shaped breast for breastfeeding.

LARGE BREASTS

If you have large breasts, it will be necessary for you and your baby to support them from underneath while feeding. Otherwise the weight of the breast will drag it down and out of the baby's mouth, causing frustration for the baby and possible nipple damage. Also, the lower part of the breast might not be drained well if it is not supported, which could lead to milk being impacted in the ducts and the breast becoming sore and inflamed (see pages 64–66).

A simple way of supporting your breast is to cup one hand underneath it. Alternatively, you can make yourself a sling out of fabric, and slip this under the breast and over your head, raising the breast slightly. An ideal feeding position for heavy breasts is to tuck the baby under your arm so that her legs are pointing behind you, and cup her head in your hand (see pages 26–27).

SMALL BREASTS

If your breasts are small, you may need to lift your baby up to the breast so that she can latch on more easily. This is easily done by laying the baby on a cushion on your lap.

BREAST SURGERY

If you have had breast surgery, some parts of the breast may not function as well as before and you will need to achieve good drainage of milk to prevent the breasts from becoming overfull. Even so, women who have had breast surgery often breastfeed with success (see page 156).

DIMPLED NIPPLES

Dimpled or inverted nipples look like dimples— they point in instead of out. If you have nipples of this type, it will be harder for your baby to draw them into the back of her mouth, and you

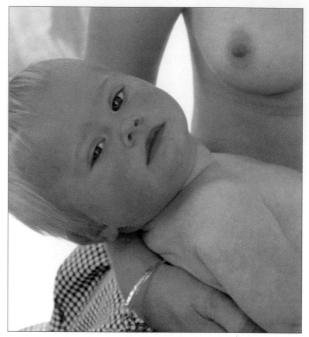

Most babies find small breasts (above) *easy to grasp, drawing the nipple to the back of the mouth and latching on to the breast's glandular tissue. If you have large nipples (below) it can be more difficult for the baby to get a firm latch, so make sure her mouth is wide open.*

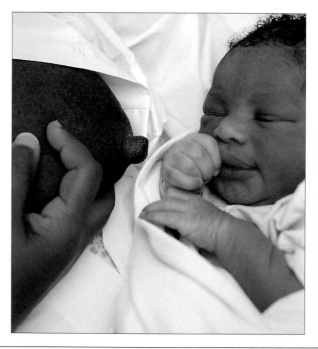

Nipples may be small *(above) or large (below). Since the baby needs to suck at the breast, not the nipple, the exact size and shape is not important, provided that the mother knows how to help her baby latch on so that the jaw firmly grasps the breast's glandular tissue.*

Mothers may have small areolas *(above) or large ones (below), but this does not affect breastfeeding. When a baby latches on and sucks at the breast, the action of the jaw molds the breast and nipples, which are composed of flexible tissue, to a shape and size to suit her mouth.*

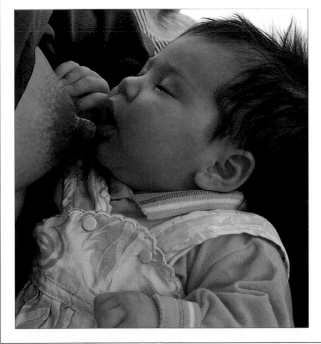

will need patience and persistence in the first ten days or so, to make sure that she gets a complete mouthful of breast every time she feeds. But if you always ensure that she has a good latch, her strong sucking will then shape and draw out the nipples so that they are adapted to her needs.

Women with dimpled nipples often approach breastfeeding feeling that they are bound to fail. Some women are even warned by people who are supposed to be helping them that their breasts are "no good" for breastfeeding, which of course places them under stress even before they lift their babies into their arms.

Many women have little confidence in their bodies, and when this is so, breastfeeding may seem like a display of magic, a kind of conjuring trick that we're unlikely to succeed at, especially if other people suggest that our breasts or nipples are the "wrong" shape. In fact, all nipples change shape in response to the natural rush of hormones in the bloodstream. Falling in love with your baby and wanting to cuddle and breastfeed her involves just such a hormone surge. So all your positive feelings about breastfeeding, the longing to hold your baby in your arms, your physical pleasure in the roundness of her head, her silky skin, her plump cheeks, and tiny fingers will all contribute to the physical changes that take place to enable you to breastfeed.

REMEDIES FOR DIMPLED NIPPLES

One simple way of producing a more pronounced nipple shape is to wrap several ice cubes in a towel and hold this to your nipple. Or keep a small spray bottle filled with water in the fridge and squirt a few shots onto your nipples before feeding your baby.

Another remedy is to circle the areola with a finger and lightly stroke the nipple. Or, if you need a stronger stimulus, try using a breast pump to express a little milk (see pages 138–39) before feeding. This will draw out the nipple and soften the area around it, making it easier for the baby to latch on. The best remedy for dimpled nipples, however, is correct positioning of the baby at the breast. Once you have got that right, the baby is in control and will mold your nipples to a perfect shape.

DIMPLED NIPPLES

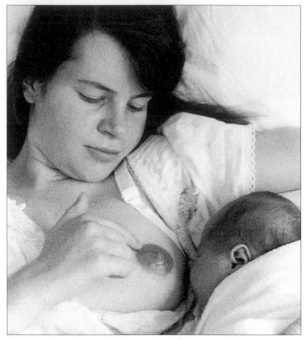

1 *Circle a finger lightly around the areola to stimulate the dimpled nipple to emerge.*

2 *Then, stroke the nipple gently with your finger. It should become more prominent.*

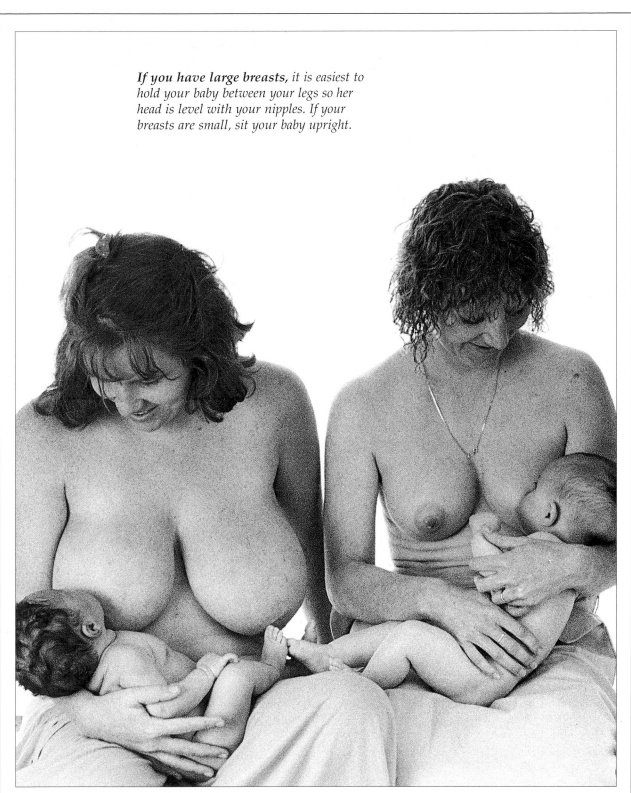

If you have large breasts, it is easiest to hold your baby between your legs so her head is level with your nipples. If your breasts are small, sit your baby upright.

THE BABY COMES TO THE BREAST

The Minutes After Birth

THE IDEAL TIME TO PUT YOUR BABY to the breast is within the first hour after birth. It is an important part of the way you welcome your baby into life and you both start to get to know each other. The baby's sucking reflex is especially strong during that first hour. If this time is missed, a baby often loses desire to suck for the next 24 hours, seems clueless when you try to put him to the breast, or may fuss and fume as if you were trying to force on him something particularly unpleasant.

Giving a baby bottles during the first hour after birth, even if they only contain water, also reduces the baby's urge to suck at the breast. In some circumstances, a baby may then have to be taught how to latch on and suckle effectively.

RESPONDING TO YOUR BABY

On the other hand, you do not have to get your baby to the breast within a specified number of minutes after birth; there is no race to do it. Nor should it turn into a performance to show that you can do it, or a duty thrust on you by other people who want to get it over and done with so that they can clean up and sign off. The important thing is simply to watch the baby carefully and respond when he signals that he wants to suck.

Some babies whose mothers have received Demerol are sleepy and not ready to suck. You need to be patient and gentle. There is no point in trying to force a baby on the breast. You may well be sleepy, too, and if you give yourself a chance to rest a bit and to come to terms with the momentous drama that has occurred, you will be in a better state to enjoy introducing your baby to the breast. Research shows that babies without Demerol in their bloodstreams may be sufficiently alert to "creep" up their mother's body to the breast—babies in a Demerol haze need time to come around.

As you hold your baby immediately after birth, you may notice that he starts to make sucking noises. As he looks around with evident interest at this new world, or gazes up in concentration at your face, he gets a bit fussy, as if there is something else he wants that would make it all perfect. He screws up his mouth, his lips twitch, he turns his head from side to side, and he may start to cry. These are all signals that he is ready to come to the breast.

Unfortunately, some babies are set aside in a crib in the early minutes and hours following the birth, so their readiness to suck goes unnoticed. But a baby in his mother's arms makes his wishes quite clear so that they can be acted on at just the right moment.

If your baby is very drowsy, he may benefit from stimulation to help him discover what he wants. Cuddling, stroking, and talking to him and having him in body contact with you provides this loving stimulation, and he will wake up and seek the breast when he is ready for it.

TRIGGERING MILK PRODUCTION

Putting a baby to the breast elicits a flow of two hormones—oxytocin and prolactin—which work together to stimulate milk production. Oxytocin causes muscle contractions and has an important function in breastfeeding, as it squeezes muscles in the milk ducts, leading to milk ejection. It also makes the uterus contract, so breastfeeding soon after birth helps the uterus tighten and prevents hemorrhage.

Oxytocin is produced more readily when you are feeling good about yourself and experiencing physical pleasure. It has been called the "happiness hormone" and the "hormone of love."* Holding your naked baby against your skin is part of the joy and sensuous delight that stimulate this hormone. It works naturally for you, so that breastfeeding starts in a state of

Within minutes of birth, the baby, still wet and warm from your womb, may already be searching for your breast (above). This meeting is for you both a sanctuary and a homecoming after the storm of labor. You enjoy skin-to-skin contact and gaze into each other's eyes for a long time in fascination (inset).

physical pleasure. The milk supply has to do with what is going on in our minds—with intense feelings and the power of emotions that flood our whole being—and not only with technique.

The other hormone, prolactin, prepares your breasts for milk production, and is secreted as a response to the baby's sucking, so that milk can flow. High prolactin levels, resulting from full and frequent breastfeeding, usually prevent a woman's getting pregnant. Prolactin, in fact, is the most widely used contraceptive in the world—though it is not a reliable one. Knowing that your baby can suck, feeling the strong tug of the jaw, and realizing that you have the right

food in your breasts to sustain the life of your baby will help you to feel confident and strong about your mothering abilities. Feeling that breastfeeding is going well can be a huge psychological boost in the early days.

Bring the baby to your breast when his mouth is gaping, as if in a yawn. If you are slow about this, his mouth may begin to close again and he cannot latch on. Aim his nose toward the nipple, so that he slightly extends his head, lifts his chin against your breast, and presses his nose against it, too. You can support his head with your hand—either the hand of the cradling arm, or, for greater ease of movement, your other hand.

A BABY'S FIRST FEED

1 *After giving birth in the water, a mother holds her baby, cradling him in the crook of her arm, and he starts rooting eagerly for the breast.*

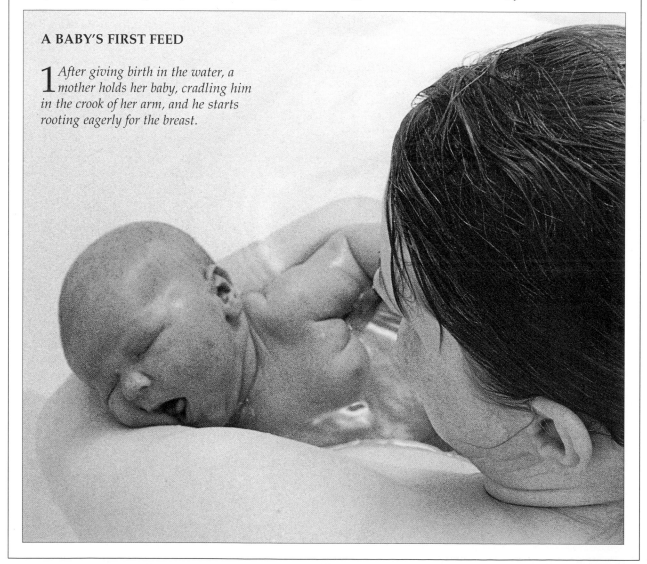

2 *Still in the water, she nestles her baby against her so that he can suckle. He seems to know immediately what to do and sucks strongly.*

The First Few Days

In the first few days after the birth you and your baby are both beginning to learn about each other—starting to get into step together as if performing an intricate dance. At first there are bound to be some missteps and when you notice them, you will change your behavior so that you find the rhythm again. As you start to develop confidence in your relationship with your baby, you will do the right things quite spontaneously. Many of these rhythms you and your baby learn together have to do with breastfeeding. Though some babies take to the breast like ducklings to water, many have to learn exactly how to latch on, if sucking is to be a satisfying experience. Mothers, too, usually have to learn how to help their babies best.

FIRST MILK

You may have noticed a slight dampness around your nipples in late pregnancy, or drops of moisture seeping from them if you were wearing a bra that was too tight and pressing on your breasts. This is colostrum, the first milk to appear in your breasts. Gradually, over the next few days, it gives way to mature milk. Some women express a little colostrum regularly in the last weeks of pregnancy, because they are told that this clears the ducts. There is no need to express colostrum for this reason, but it may help you feel confident about breastfeeding if you can see that you actually have a working system. A few drops are enough.

Colostrum has unique properties. It is higher in protein and lower in fat and carbohydrates than mature milk, so the baby needs very little to get off to a good nutritional start. It also contains a higher proportion of substances that protect the baby from infection. Even though your baby is getting only small quantities of colostrum, you are helping her to build up a strong immunological defense system. Colostrum, like more mature breastmilk, will give your baby all she needs in the early days of life. It is a laxative, too, ensuring that the meconium, or feces, in the baby's bowel

LEARNING TO BREASTFEED

1 It may seem that your breasts are very large and the baby very small (above). You wonder how she can open her mouth wide enough to latch on.

2 But she succeeds in latching on and sucks energetically (opposite), and together you begin the rhythm of breastfeeding.

is cleared out quickly. If this process is delayed, a baby is more likely to suffer from jaundice (see page 101), probably because meconium is reabsorbed through the intestinal walls.

PRODUCING ENOUGH MILK

It is particularly important to resist giving any supplements to your baby in the first few days. Offering a bottle of artificial milk or boiled water will reduce the frequency of sucking and the time the baby spends at the breast. Feed whenever your baby asks for milk, and for as long as she wishes. Production of breastmilk is dependent on the frequency, intensity, and duration of sucking. So if you want to get your milk flowing well, and to produce a generous quantity, put the baby to the breast as often as you can.

A satisfying feeding over, the mother holds her baby close in a loving embrace. The baby is completely relaxed, her whole body soft and loose, and her head heavy.

Stress can interfere with the milk ejection reflex and impede milk flow, so in the first few days especially, while you are still new to breastfeeding, relax and take your time:

• Select a peaceful setting.
• Find a comfortable position, with good back support.
• Do not hurry. You have all the time in the world.
• Pick up the baby before she gets fretful.
• Drop your shoulders, breathe out, and relax as you put the baby to the breast. While the baby is feeding, keep your shoulders and arms loose, and breathe slowly and regularly.
• Ensure that the baby is latched on to the breast, not the nipple.
• Focus mentally on the visual image of your milk flowing into the baby.
• Have a glass of water or juice beside you to sip if you feel thirsty.
• If noises interfere with your focus on breastfeeding, create a musical barrier using your tape player or radio.
• Do not interrupt your time with the baby at the breast for anything or anyone.
• If necessary, take the phone off the hook, put a notice on your door saying "Mother and baby resting, please do not disturb," or have someone shield you from intrusions.

YOUR FEELINGS

In Western cultures breastfeeding is an unfamiliar sight for many people. Often a first-time mother has never sat with other breastfeeding women, so she has not had a chance to see how they handle their babies and what the babies do. Breastfeeding can seem like a difficult technical performance, or even a complicated conjuring trick.

If your mother was unable to breastfeed you, or you do not have friends who have breastfed easily, you may have many doubts about it and be concerned that you cannot produce enough milk. In many countries breastfeeding is still taken for granted, and women breastfeed not only because it is the safest and easiest way to feed babies, but because they have never seriously considered doing it any other way. In industrial countries, however, pregnant women often say that they will "try" to breastfeed their babies. They are preprogrammed for failure.

This is so not only because women often lack self-confidence but also because the manufacturers of artificial milk advertise "special" baby formulas with photographs of robust babies thriving on their products. Nobody advertises a mother's milk, but it is, without doubt, the best milk for her baby, being exactly suited to her baby's needs.

Women often do not trust their bodies to make milk. In many ways our bodies may have been a nuisance to us—such as when we have had to cope with the physical changes of adolescence, with menstruation and contraception, and, not least, with pregnancy and birth. If the birth was complicated, it is an added reason why we might feel unsure about our bodies. But when milk starts to be produced and you can see it dripping out and the baby enjoying it, your body suddenly starts to make sense. This experience is especially important for any woman who has disliked her body in the past. Then, breastfeeding comes to her almost as a revelation.

FEAR OF BEING DRAINED

Breastfeeding may arouse very deep emotions. When the baby comes to the breast and sucks with vigor, it can feel as if you are in danger of being eaten up. Women who are having difficulties with breastfeeding often say they feel drained, and the baby is sucking out their energy. Yet the energy required to shop for, sterilize, prepare, warm, and give bottles of formula is more than that needed to lift a baby to the breast, cuddle her, and let your own milk flow.

The real root of this fear of being drained or consumed by the baby lies more with the seemingly impossible demands for love and care made on women—with energy being used up in nurturing other people, and having no time or energy for ourselves. When a baby kicks, punches, scratches, and bites you, you may feel you are being attacked, but it is important not to respond as if to an enemy. You need to show the baby that you survive these attacks, and are still there, constant and unchanged. In this way you reveal to your baby what love is.

Feeding Positions

There are several different feeding positions you can adopt; over time if you experiment, you will soon discover which is the most comfortable. Whatever position you choose, it is important that you be relaxed, as this will encourage the flow of milk.

THE "FRENCH LOAF HOLD"

A newborn baby should be held to the breast so that he faces it full on. This will make it easier for him to latch on correctly. The best way to do this is to tuck the baby under your arm on the side you will be feeding so that his legs are pointing behind you, and cradle his head in your hand. Then you can guide him gently to the breast. Alternatively, you can support the baby across your lap and hold the head with your free hand. Avoid putting pressure against the top of the baby's head, as this will make him lift his chin so that he is in a nibbling, rather than a suckling, position.

New mothers are often told to press the breast near the baby's nose to allow him to breathe. There is rarely any need for this, however, as babies' nostrils are conveniently flared, so that even when their mouths are stuffed full with delicious breast, they can breathe easily. In fact, if you try to press the breast, it may accidentally push the nipple away from the back of the baby's mouth by deforming the sphere of the breast. Once the baby is adept at positioning himself at the breast, and you are more confident with feeding, you will be able to experiment with other positions.

DIFFERENT POSITIONS

Most women feed their babies while sitting in a chair, as this is the most convenient position. But you can also lie on your side with the baby next to you, which can be more comfortable if you have had stitches. Or you can sit cross-legged, thus forming a natural cradle for your baby. As long as you are relaxed and well supported, any feeding position is a good one.

One way to hold a new baby is to tuck her body under your arm so that she is facing you, and cradle her head with your hand (left). You can support your breast with the free hand (inset). Imagine that you are holding three or four French loaves under your arm, grasping their ends with your hand placed underneath. It may be easiest to support a small baby on a pillow. This position is good after a cesarean birth.

ALTERNATIVE POSITIONS

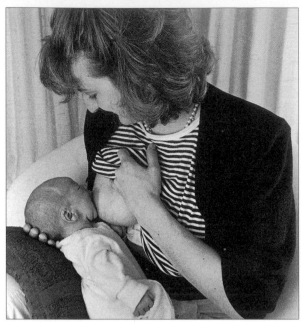

One way to nurse a tiny baby *is to place her on a cushion on your lap, and guide her head to the breast with your hand.*

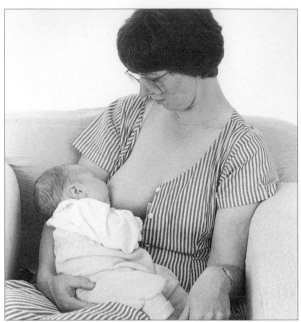

Sit a small baby upright *on your lap so that she can reach the breast more easily. Support her head and back with your arm.*

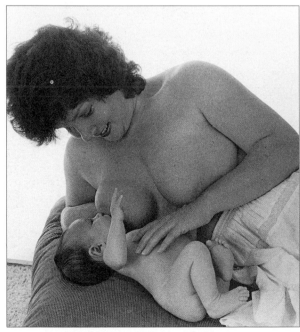

A semi-reclining position *is a good way to nurse your baby after a cesarean birth, but make sure you have pillows supporting your back and head.*

To nurse an older baby, *sit on a low chair with one knee raised higher than the other to form a natural slope for your baby to lie on.*

Sit cross-legged on the floor and cradle your baby with both arms. This position is very comfortable and makes your baby feel secure.

An older child will snuggle up to you in a position comfortable to her. Sit against firm cushions for complete relaxation.

One way of feeding twins is to sit comfortably in a chair with a baby at each breast. Make sure that your arms are well supported by cushions.

To nurse two children at the same time, lay them across your lap so that the smallest child is on top of the other. Make sure you have firm back support.

Latching On

The most important element in breastfeeding is knowing how to get the baby correctly latched on to your breast. Once you can achieve that, everything else will follow naturally. Nearly all the problems women meet in breastfeeding—sore nipples, not having enough milk, engorgement, blocked milk ducts, mastitis, breast abscess, and having a baby crying constantly with hunger—occur because their babies are not latched on well in the first place.

FINDING THE RIGHT TIME
Though most babies take to suckling as readily as newborn kittens, there are some—equally intelligent—who don't seem to know what they are being offered and do not immediately latch on. And there are a few who, even after they have latched on, are slow to make the association between this and sucking. As a general rule, babies will not respond positively to being put to the breast if they are very sleepy or if they are crying frantically. There is a special state of readiness for sucking, when the baby is alert and eager but not desperate. You will know it when you see it. If some days have passed since birth, and you still have not succeeded in getting your baby to enjoy the breast, you can start by feeding her expressed milk.

FEEDING WITH EXPRESSED MILK
Stimulate your supply of milk by sponging your breasts with warm water, gently massaging them, and expressing some milk every three hours or so (see pages 136–39). The exact timing is not important, but it should be done regularly.

THE LACTATING BREAST

Milk ducts carry milk *from the milk-producing glands to the nipple. The milk reaches the baby via tiny openings in the nipple like holes in a watering can nozzle.*

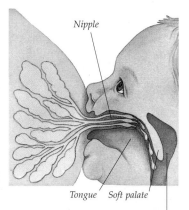

Fatty tissue
Milk duct
Nipple
Milk producing gland
Rib

Milk-producing gland

Milk-producing cell
Muscle wall
Milk duct

THE SUCKING EFFECT

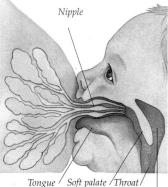

Nipple
Tongue / Soft palate / Throat
Open nasal cavity

The baby grasps the glandular tissue *with her jaw and, with each suck, presses the front of her tongue against the base of the nipple which is drawn deep into the mouth (left). The back of her tongue presses up against the soft palate (below left), which is raised to seal off the nasal cavity as milk flows into the throat for her to swallow (below).*

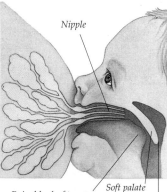

Nipple
Raised back of tongue
Soft palate
Closed nasal cavity

Nipple
Tongue   Soft palate
Nasal cavity

When you are ready to put your baby to the breast, first satisfy her initial hunger by giving her a little of your milk from a sterilized teaspoon or bottle. If you choose a bottle, select a teat which is shaped like a real nipple, so that your nipple will not be such a surprise for your baby when she encounters it. After she has had one or two ounces of milk—not more—and is ready to stop for a moment to catch her breath, it is the right time to try to interest her in the breast.

HELPING YOUR BABY TO LATCH ON

Place the baby on your lap, her tummy against yours, and tease her with your fingers or your nipple, touching the sides of her mouth to let her know that something exciting is going to happen. Some babies will respond by rooting. Others will look as if they do not know what you are doing. Either way, watch for the moment when your baby opens her mouth wide, and then move her head firmly against the breast so that her lower jaw holds the underneath arc of the areola and the nipple slides deep into her mouth.

A GOOD LATCH

To help your baby get a good latch you can use the "French loaf hold," with the baby's legs tucked under your arm on the same side and your cupped hand cradling her head and shoulders (see page 26).

Alternatively, you can place the baby on your lap, cradle her in your arms, or put her on a pillow on your knee. If you prefer this, she should not have to twist her head to take the breast. Make sure that you are tummy to tummy. It will then be easy for your baby to latch on.

Be aware of the signs that your baby is ready for a feed. It is not only a matter of crying, and it is best not to wait until a baby is distressed, for she may be too frantic to get well latched on.

A baby has powerful built-in survival skills, and when ready for a feed seeks the breast with urgency and impatience, making movements that help her latch on correctly. With mouth agape, like a hungry chick, the baby comes to the breast, breathing rapidly and obviously excited. She is ready to achieve the perfect latch.

Right on target, the baby clasps the breast with strong jaws so that the nipple slides deep into his mouth, and he feels the pleasure of the contact between the nipple and palate. Now that he is well latched on, he can suck vigorously to stimulate the flow of milk—the feast begins!

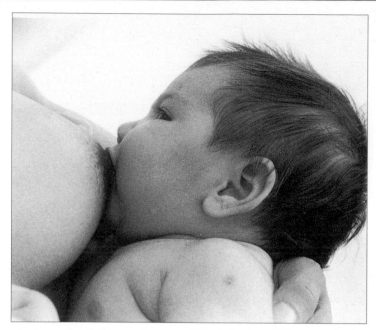

An incorrect latch can happen if the baby is positioned too high on the breast (above). Her mouth is not open wide enough to grasp the breast tissues firmly, with her tongue and lower jaw so she is sucking at the nipple rather than the breast (see below). This will make the nipple sore, and the baby will soon be hungry again because she will only be able to reach the low-calorie foremilk, which is thirst-quenching, and not the rich, creamy hindmilk.

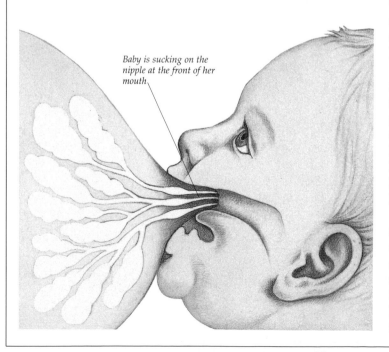

Baby is sucking on the nipple at the front of her mouth

PATIENCE AND PERSEVERANCE

If she latches, it is as if in one instant you have both got it right. If she does not latch, she will slide off easily. Then you do it again, and, if necessary, again and again until you get it right.

If your baby starts to fuss and cry, as she is very likely to do, change her position radically, holding her upright over your shoulder or on her tummy on your lap, and soothe her into a state where you can start again. Talk to her reassuringly, letting her know by the tone of your voice that you are confident she will get it right. If necessary, hand her to someone else while you breathe out, drop your shoulders, relax, and calm down.

When your baby is at the breast, you cannot see whether her lower jaw is well down, grasping breast tissue. But you can feel when her jaw is way below your nipple. This is how it is with a good latch, when the baby has a good mouthful, with two-thirds breast and only one-third nipple.

Babies are conveniently snub-nosed, with receding chins and flared nostrils, so they can breathe freely when they are at the breast, even if their faces look squashed.

As the baby is about to suck, her mouth opens wide. There is a moment's pause, and then you feel the grasp of her jaw as she presses on the alveoli (milk sacs), and know that she has obtained a mouthful of milk, having been able to use the pressure of her tongue to squirt it into the back of her throat and swallow it.

Occasionally a baby becomes confused and manages to get her tongue over the nipple, rather than underneath it, so she cannot possibly use her tongue effectively. If this happens, use your pinkie to release her mouth from your nipple, and try to latch her on again.

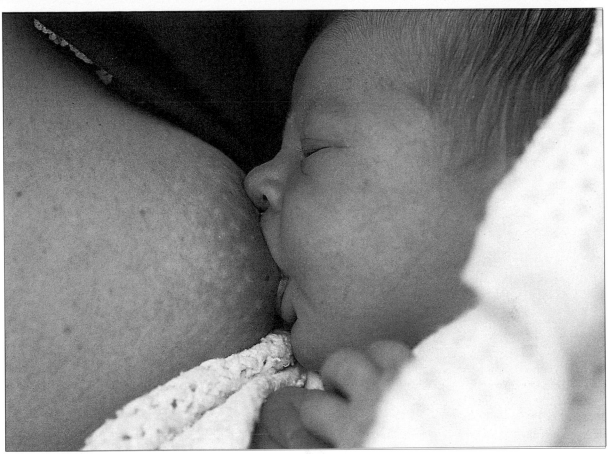

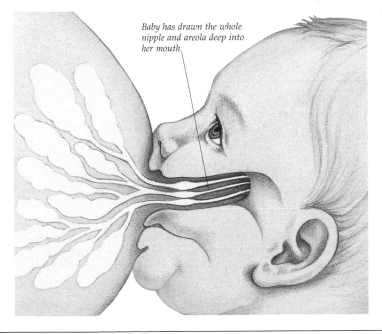

Baby has drawn the whole nipple and areola deep into her mouth

A correct latch allows the baby to suckle on the breast (above) rather than the nipple alone. Her mouth is wide open and her lower jaw holds the lower arc of the areola. This enables her to get a good mouthful of breast so that she can pump the milk with her jaws and tongue from deep inside the breast. The nipple is drawn deep into the baby's mouth (left) so that it is pressed between the tongue and the palate, enabling her to suck well. This stimulates the milk ejection reflex and milk flows freely.

A mother encourages one of her twins to latch on, while the other sucks his fingers, awaiting his turn. It is often easier to feed twins one at a time than to struggle to get them both latched on simultaneously.

BABIES AT THE BREAST

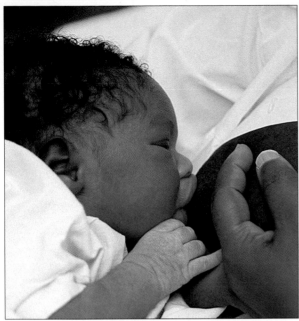

Oblivious to all but the pleasure of warm, sweet milk, a baby who is well latched on to the breast settles down to a satisfying feed. His mother can see the muscle above and in front of his ear working.

BIG AND SMALL NIPPLES

Women are sometimes anxious that their nipples are too small. In fact, big nipples can be more of a problem, because a newborn baby with a small mouth may not be able to get a good mouthful of breast tissue and so press on the milk sinuses.

It is very frustrating for a baby to suck when no milk flows. The baby starts to fuss, and then the mother becomes anxious and confused. Her distress is communicated to the baby, who responds by becoming flustered and uncoordinated. They get into a vicious circle.

The solution may be for the mother to press hot towels against her breast immediately before feeding, and then to massage her breast and use firm but gentle hand pressure to help the milk spurt out, thus encouraging the baby to use a jaw movement to pump the milk. A baby often needs the experience of only one good feed to be able to figure out how to do it. A mother, too, gains enormous confidence when things go right, and this confidence is the basis for acquiring the art of breastfeeding. Even if things don't go well the first few times, you will know that if you can get it right once, you can do it again.

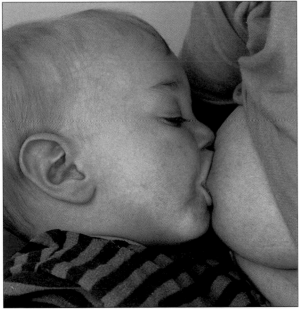

When experiencing the rush of milk heralded by the milk ejection reflex, a baby is in a state of concentrated sensuous satisfaction.

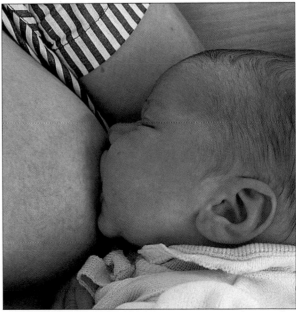

Babies have receding chins, which makes it easy for them to fill their mouths with breast without any obstructions.

Getting Help with Latching On

If your baby finds it difficult to latch on, you may want someone to help you put him to the breast. This could be your midwife, your partner, or a breastfeeding counselor. First, position yourself comfortably, either lying on your side supported by pillows, with your upper knee bent so that your back and shoulders are rounded, or sitting up with your back well supported. For a right-handed woman, feeding from the left breast is usually easier, at least to start with.

If your baby is not desperate to be fed, take a little time for breast massage while someone else holds the baby and keeps him happy. Apply a comfortably hot towel to your breast for about 15 seconds. Then express some milk by hand (see page 137). Continue stimulating the breast until you can see pearl-like drops of milk glistening on the nipple. Now you can relax, knowing that milk is ready and waiting for your baby.

THE HELPER'S ROLE

Your helper sits at the same level by your side, facing you, and holds the baby so that the heel of her right palm presses against the baby's upper back and shoulders, and her spread thumb and first finger of that hand supports the base of the back of the baby's head. With her other hand, your helper lifts your left breast to the level of the baby's nose and at the same time, with her right hand, guides the baby's head so it is facing the breast, with the mouth slightly below the level of the nipple.

In order to draw the lower arc of the areola and the nipple into his mouth, the baby has to lift his chin. It is impossible for a baby to open his mouth wide enough to latch on if his chin is not lifted, because then there will be insufficient space for vigorous jaw movement. As soon as the baby's mouth opens wide and the chin is well raised, your helper lifts your breast into the baby's mouth, introducing the nipple deeply, and tilting it upward so that it presses against

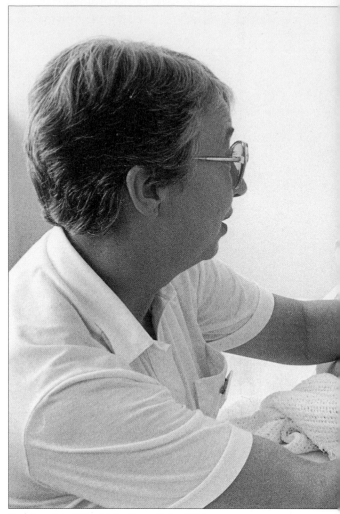

the back of the baby's palate. This requires careful timing and coordination of movement: the baby's open mouth has to meet the center of the breast at exactly the same moment as the breast is lifted into the baby's mouth. While the baby sucks, the helper continues to hold the breast about two inches away from the areola, and presses in on the glandular tissue. If the baby has not latched on well, the helper moves him back in order to try again.

She may have to do this several times to get the latch right. Some babies are patient about this, while others get very cross. If your baby becomes furious, the helper should pick him up and cuddle and talk to him until he is soothed before trying again. If he is crying and upset,

THE MIDWIFE HELPS

1 A midwife rests the baby on a cushion on the mother's lap, cradles the back of his head in one hand, and holds the breast in the other hand.

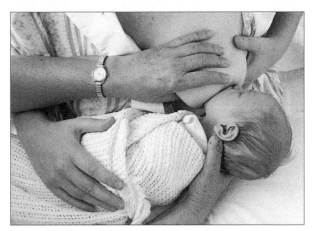

2 She waits for his mouth to open wide, then latches him firmly on to the breast.

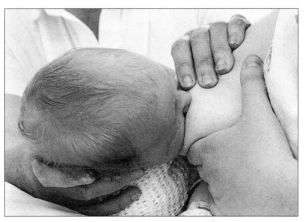

3 The mother supports her breast underneath, well back from the areola, with one hand.

4 Now the mother latches the baby on by herself, supporting his back with her right arm.

you will get upset, too, and your baby will be so angry that he will be too distracted to respond to the stimulus of the breast.

If the helper mistakenly presses in on the areola, rather than the breast, the position is bound to be wrong. This results in only the nipple entering the baby's mouth. To suck well, a baby needs a good mouthful of breast.

Once the baby is in a good sucking rhythm, the helper removes her hand from the breast and the baby will stay latched on. He will pause in his sucking occasionally and then continue as energetically as before. Let the baby go at his own pace. Remember to talk encouragingly to him all the time and tell him how clever he is and how much you love him.

AND NOW YOU'RE ON YOUR OWN

1 *The baby enjoys lying naked (left), free to explore her mother's breast. She gazes into her mother's eyes and her whole body becomes excited. The mother, in turn, gets pleasure from exciting her baby. Her breasts become hot and her nipples firm.*

2 *Now the baby roots for the breast (top right), turning her head from side to side, opening her mouth to grasp the breast. The mother gently restrains an eager little hand so that it cannot get in the way, and allows her breast to drop into the baby's mouth.*

3 *The baby latches on to the breast (bottom right), her jaws sealed tight, creating a vacuum. She draws the nipple deeply into her mouth and presses it against her palate. The muscles above her ears are working hard as she sucks eagerly with energy.*

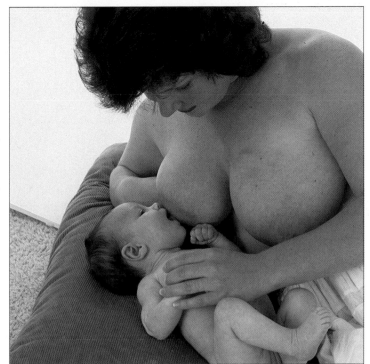

Sucking Rhythms

Imagine sitting down to a meal and having someone prodding you to keep chewing and swallowing. As soon as you paused to talk or to take a rest, this person would give your head a shove, smack your feet, bump you up and down or from side to side, or push the food impatiently into your mouth and tell you to get on with it and stop playing around. This is how feeds are for some unfortunate babies—no wonder they do not seem to enjoy them very much!

SUCKING AND SWALLOWING
Each baby has an individual sucking pattern—it is not something you can force on a baby. However, no breastfed baby sucks and swallows without pause, except in short bursts, or at the beginning of a feed when she is hungry or thirsty.

During a feed there can be from three to fourteen "chomps," or sucks—two a second—and then a pause. The pauses last about half as long as the sucking, and are followed by another burst of sucking, and so on.

FAST FLOW OF MILK
When the milk supply is copious, which is often the case at the beginning of a feed, the baby swallows after each chomp, as she is trying to keep up with the fast flow. Or she may stop sucking entirely because milk is flooding her mouth and she needs to let it run out of the sides and down her chin. If she does not do this, she will gasp and choke on the milk.

THE END OF A FEED
When the milk ejection reflex is delayed or the supply of milk is not so generous, and at the end of a feed, there may be several chomps before the baby swallows. As a feed draws to a close, a baby may take a snooze, wake up to have a few more chomps and swallows, and then drift off again, still with a mouthful of breast. Babies often like to continue dozing and sucking intermittently for lengthy periods after their hunger is satisfied. It feels so good to be at the breast that they do

A baby pauses in midfeeding (above) to look around. He may smile at someone else, and notice interesting objects in the room. A baby at the breast learns that people are responsive—and that he has the power to make them respond. Then he grasps the breast firmly with his jaw and returns to nurse with fresh energy and enthusiasm.

During another pause in feeding, the baby looks up into his mother's eyes (opposite), his tongue still in the sucking position and his mouth full of milk. She smiles and speaks and he smiles and coos in return. Babies do not suck continuously without interruption. Once the initial hunger and thirst are satisfied, there is time for a brief pause. It is an opportunity for satisfying preverbal conversation, and it is often the occasion when a baby first smiles and coos. This is the beginning of language.

not want to let go. If you have other things you want to do, and there is no one else around to entertain her, try putting her down with exciting objects to watch or music to listen to, or you could try snuggling her up in a baby sling. You will soon learn what your baby likes best, and how looking in a mirror, having a bath, playing with a rattle, or being taken for a walk can mollify her for the temporary loss of the breast.

You may be aware that you have more than one milk ejection reflex during a feed, because, for example, the feed is interrupted for social reasons, the baby needs her diaper changed, or because she has a brief nap in the middle. You feel a second or even a third rush of milk, and this will change the baby's sucking pattern as milk pours afresh into her mouth.

The pattern of sucking also varies between day and night. Fortunately, when you are rested and relaxed in the middle of the night, the baby is likely to suck regularly and be ready to settle down after a short feed—especially if there is nothing exciting to attract her attention. In the early morning, too, when you have a copious milk supply, she may suck eagerly and then fall asleep again, or else sit happily and play.

THE SOCIAL FEEDS
It is later in the day, especially in the early evening, when you may have the long, leisurely feeds in which the baby clings to your breast like a barnacle on a rock. These feeds are characterized by quick bursts of sucking followed by an occasional swallow and then a doze. You may feel

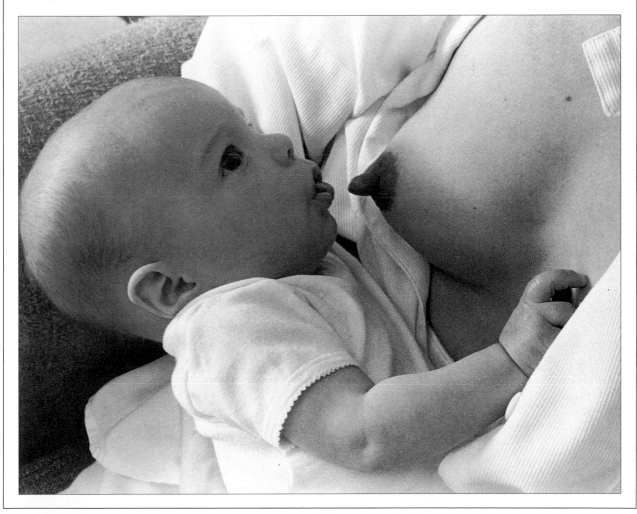

that you will never be able to pry the baby off the breast—even to go to the bathroom, answer the door, or make a cup of tea for yourself. When a baby is adept at clinging on, come hell or high water, do not just pull her away or you will make your nipple sore. Instead, slip your pinkie into the corner of her mouth to break the vacuum created by her sucking.

These lengthy feeds, in which there are a variety of sucking rhythms, are also the social feeds—the ones in which a great deal of communication is going on between your baby and you. That is why they are so valuable. What is taking place is the start of language.

The baby slips off the breast, smiles at you, and then grabs the breast again. She pats your breast, or strokes the fabric of your shirt, then fiddles with a button or zipper, or your other nipple, and looks up to see how you feel about these things. She comes off the breast briefly to inspect it visually, and then darts forward to grasp it in her mouth again. She fixes you with her gaze, sucking slows down, the nipple slips

out of her mouth, and she coos and gurgles—but only for a moment. Then she homes in on it again and begins sucking vigorously and earnestly. Try to be leisurely about at least one or two feeds in the 24 hours; you can both enjoy and benefit from this social interchange.

MOTHER AND BABY DIALOGUE

Breastfeeding is not all sucking and swallowing. It is about the exchange of thoughts and feelings—about being human. Mothers understand this well. While a baby is busy sucking, a mother is usually still and quiet, perhaps watching her and studying the concentration on her face. But when her baby pauses to look around or catch her breath, she starts to stroke, jiggle, or talk to her. Mothers and babies take part in a continuous dialogue in which the baby plays as big a part as the mother.

If your baby is still firmly latched on but not sucking, you can, if you wish, slide a finger into her mouth, or you can stroke the side of her mouth or lower cheeks. You will often find that

RHYTHMS OF A FEED

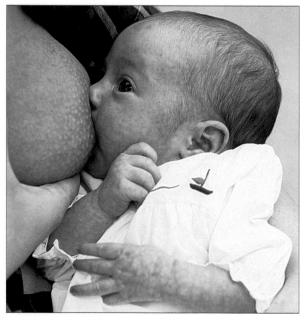

1 *At first she sucks strongly and rhythmically, but when she is getting full, the sucking slows down, and she may doze off occasionally.*

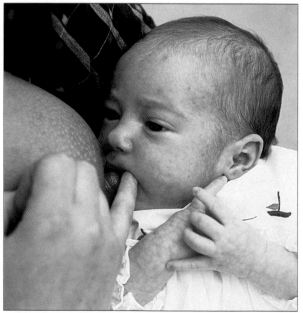

2 *If she is still firmly latched on, but not sucking, and you want to be able to put her down, slip a finger into her mouth to break the vacuum.*

this stimulates her to come to the breast again eagerly until at last she slips off, satiated and completely content.

Even when it seems that a baby has had a satisfying feed, she may want to suckle again after she has been burped. Most mothers know that when they are racing against the clock, because they have to go out, for example, this is always the time when a baby fusses after a feed and will not settle. A rushed feed is asking for trouble.

BABY-LED BREASTFEEDING
Breastfeeding should be baby-led. It is difficult to forget about time, forget about clocks, forget about other things you need to do, and focus on the baby, but aim to make breastfeeding an oasis of peace in your day.

You are not merely filling a baby up with milk. When it is going well, breastfeeding can be pleasurable, not just a job you want to do well. This is because a good breastfeeding experience raises endorphin levels. Endorphins are a form

of morphine that is released naturally by the body. They not only have an analgesic effect, but also produce an emotional "high." These are the same hormones that flood into the bloodstream when an athlete gladly pushes herself to the physical limit, that increase arousal in passionate lovemaking, and that add to the excitement of childbirth, too, when a woman feels that her body knows what it is doing, and is free to do it. Endorphins are life-enhancing. They suffuse us with warmth and a sense of fulfillment.

A woman starts to breastfeed by responding to signals given by the baby, perhaps anxiously at first, or in a slightly irritated way, because she must interrupt what she is doing. Once the baby settles at her breast, though, the mother begins to relax and live in the moment.

There is a rhythm of breastfeeding for the mother, too: the desire to meet the baby's need, then the action of putting the baby to the breast, her awareness of the buzz and tingle of the milk ejection reflex, followed by a feeling of deep satisfaction and completeness as the baby suckles.

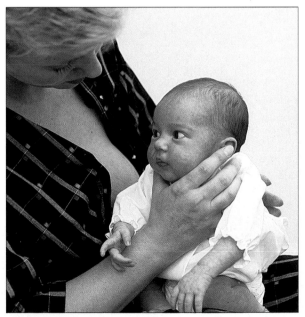

3 *Unless she is heavy with sleep, make sure she is comfortable by holding her upright again, and gently rubbing her back to see if she needs to burp.*

4 *After she has been burped, it may be that she wants to have another suck. She drops off to sleep while still at the breast, secure and satisfied.*

Night Feeds

The easiest way to feed your baby at night is to have him in bed with you. He will bask in the warmth of your body, and you can give him the breast without delay whenever he is ready for a feed. This is less disturbing for everyone within earshot than waiting for him to cry.

It helps to have a wide bed, as you have more room to maneuver when feeding. Lay the baby directly on the mattress rather than using a pillow. There is no danger of suffocation for a healthy baby in a big bed—he will turn his head from side to side and move away if something blocks his nostrils and prevents him from breathing.

It has been suggested that babies benefit from the stimulus to breathing that comes from exhaled carbon dioxide—something they only get if they are close to other people, and that some crib deaths occur because babies sleeping alone don't have this chemical respiratory stimulus. Whether or not this is so, babies enjoy being cuddled up to a soft, enfolding body, and they like to be able to reach the breast without fuss or delay.

If you choose not to have your baby in bed with you, you can keep him in the same room while he still needs feeding at night, so that you can reach him quickly. Obviously, it is unwise for a couple to have a baby in bed with them if they are taking sleeping pills or other drugs, or have been drinking heavily.

ENCOURAGING YOUR BABY TO SLEEP

If you want to persuade your baby that nighttime is for sleep, rather than a lively social occasion, it is a good idea to keep lights off, avoid talking in a stimulating way, let your movements be slow and gentle, and stay drowsy and relaxed yourself—this may all come naturally, of course—and unless your baby is soaking, or has a sore bottom, don't bother to change his diaper.

Some people cope well with disturbed nights and find it easy to fall asleep after feeding the baby, and wake refreshed after only a few hours' sleep. Others feel dreadful. If your partner is sleeping solidly while you have to wake two or three times a night to feed your baby, you may feel resentful and angry. After a week or so, you may also be exhausted. Talk this over with your partner and suggest that he give one of these feeds in the form of expressed milk from a bottle. This will give you an extra two to three hours' solid sleep and restore some much-needed energy.

Tuck your baby up cosily between you both, without any pillows. He will turn his head from side to side and breathe and move easily, without being impeded by bedding, and you will be aware of his rhythmic breathing and know when he wants to suck again.

If you sit up in bed to feed your baby at night, make sure your back is well supported. It helps to have a pile of firm pillows to lean against. After you have finished feeding, throw the pillows out of the bed and tuck your baby up beside you.

A relaxing way to feed your baby is to lie half on your side, supporting him in the crook of your arm. Since this is such a comfortable position, you may fall asleep with your baby still at the breast and wake to find him nestling against you.

If you are working outside the home and have your baby fed with bottles of either expressed milk or formula during the time you are separated, evening and nighttime feeds are important to ensure an abundant milk supply. If a baby is not gaining weight, take him to bed with you and breastfeed whenever he stirs.

Night feeds also play an important part in your continuing close and intimate relationship with your baby. Whether you have your baby in bed with you or—if you find that the baby is restless and disturbs you—right next to your bed, you simply cuddle him up whenever he indicates that he wants the breast. In the morning, you may not be able to say how many feeds your baby has had, and you certainly won't know for how long, because breastfeeding has merged with sleep and with milky, comforting dreams.

If your baby is beside you, he will not have to cry before you put him to the breast. You will notice his little movements as he lifts his hands to his face, turns his head from side to side, and makes sucking noises. This is your signal to put him to the breast.

Breastfeeding at night raises your prolactin levels. Prolactin is the hormone that stimulates milk-producing cells. Prolactin also helps you relax, and you may sleep better than ever before.

KEEPING YOUR BABY SAFE
It is best if the baby lies on his back on a smooth, flat surface. If you have only a small bed that is a tight squeeze for three of you, or if you have soft pillows and a heavy comforter or thick blankets, the baby's airways could become obstructed if he wriggles. You will also want to avoid letting the baby become overheated. Do not overdress your baby at night. A bed that might feel comfortably warm for you could be too hot for a baby who is snuggled down right under the bedding. Remember that your own body heat is providing natural warmth as well. If you feel the back of your baby's neck, you will soon be able to tell whether your baby is getting too hot. If so, just slip some covers off.

Babies get overheated in cribs, too. It is thought that this may be one of the causes of Sudden Infant Death Syndrome (crib death). Having your baby in bed with you allows you to be aware of his body temperature in a way that you cannot be if he is in a separate bed.

A baby should never have to breathe in cigarette smoke. It is vital that no one smokes in any room where there is a baby—and certainly never in the bedroom.

MOTHER AND BABY SCENTS
When mother and baby are tucked up in bed together they both relax in each other's smell. Little is known about the satisfying and relaxing effect of scent. Yet every mother knows the particular scent of her baby, and every baby knows the special scent of his mother. Newborns can find their mother's breast and crawl to it by smell alone, rather like little pigs snuffling for truffles. From birth on, babies can distinguish between breastpads worn by women who are not their mothers and those worn by their mothers.* So it is not surprising that research shows that babies prefer unwashed to washed nipples.* When mother and baby sleep together and are cuddled up and warm at night, their body scents become intensified.

In many cultures where women breastfeed successfully, babies sleep with their mothers. It is taken for granted that this is the safest and most comfortable place for the baby to be. In Jamaica, for example, I found that mothers are often very busy during the day, so night is the special time when they are there for their babies and breastfeed generously. As a result, babies and toddlers get most of their milk, and most of their protein, during the night. This night feeding often continues long after the child is eating solid foods during the day. These babies rarely cry because the breast is offered freely.

Sleeping together makes breastfeeding simpler. Letting the baby suckle during the night boosts the mother's prolactin levels and so helps milk production, and may offer the baby increased maternal antibodies against infection.

The Barrier of Clothing

It would not be practical to always breastfeed naked, but if you do so occasionally, you will soon discover that clothing —both yours and the baby's—can act as a barrier to correct positioning of the baby at the breast, turning the whole procedure into a juggling act.

FROM BELTS TO BRAS

Wearing a thick sweater or a wide belt with a buckle at the waist can make it difficult for you to position the baby correctly against your body. A nightdress may not open up enough for easy feeding, and even those designed for maternity wear may bunch up in awkward places and get in the way.

Some bras can restrict and press in on the breast so that even when you have managed to open the trapdoor to feed through, and struggled to poke your breasts through the flaps like bulky parcels through a mail drop, the globes of the breasts are distorted. A thick seam, or cups that are too small, may press on the breast, causing continual leakage of milk and uncomfortably soggy nipples. Some bra fastenings, too, may be tricky to cope with one-handed, while bras with zips can endanger delicate breast tissue. Tight-fitting clothing might press against the breast and make the nipple point at the wrong angle—instead of being tilted up against the baby's palate, it goes in straight, as if aimed at her tonsils, making it difficult for the baby to latch on well.

Going topless would appear to be the simplest solution, but as most people wear clothes most of the time, you need to have adaptable clothes in which you can feed easily, without fuss. Loose-fitting tops such as T-shirts and sweaters are the easiest things to wear. All you have to do is lift up your top and put your baby to the breast, without having to bother with undoing buttons or coping with awkward fastenings.

BABY CLOTHES

Swaddling your baby in layers of heavy clothing and a blanket will make it hard to position her correctly. An upturned collar, or rows of buttons or frills, can all get in the way, while sweaters and cardigans can rumple up until they are bundled around the baby's neck like a scarf, preventing her jaw from moving. Steer clear of fussy clothing and be careful not to overdress your baby.

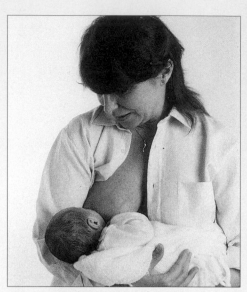

Wearing a loose shirt *makes it easy when breastfeeding. The fabric should be washable, and preferably patterned, so stains don't show.*

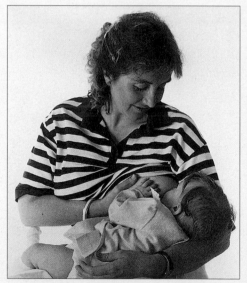

Lifting a T-shirt *involves less fuss and does not expose your breast, so it may be your choice if you want to breastfeed in a public place.*

It is lovely when you can breastfeed topless and be in close skin contact with your baby. Even if you cannot do this all the time, you may enjoy the intimacy that comes when neither of you is impeded by clothing.

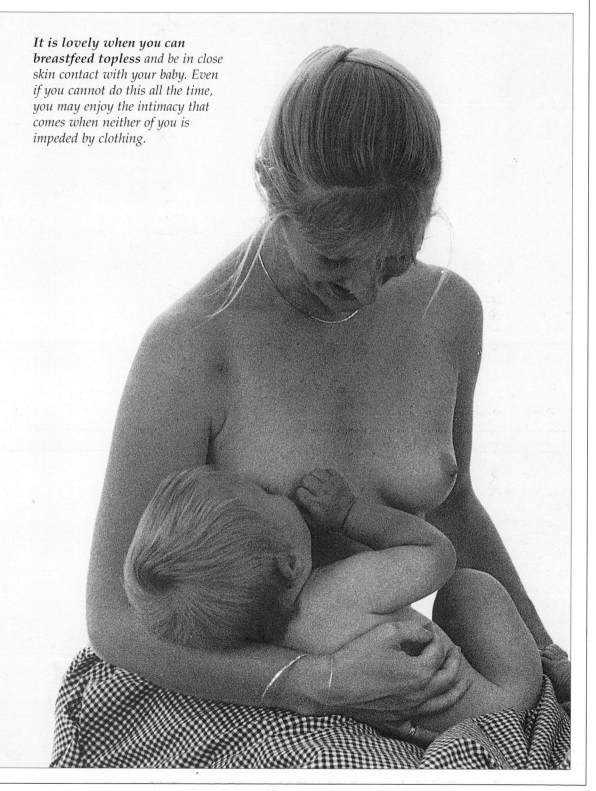

MAKING MILK

Feeding Yourself

WHEN YOU HAVE A NEW BABY you may find that you focus all your energy on the baby's needs and forget about yourself. As the weeks go by and you are busy coping with the phenomenal amount of laundry, cleaning, and constant tidying up that go hand in hand with a new baby, you might find that you skip meals or eat fast food because you are too tired to cook. When you are breastfeeding, it is very important to take care of yourself and to eat well, not only because the nutrients in what you eat pass through your milk into the baby, and not only because you have to be fit to look after a baby, but for your own sake, because you matter.

EATING SENSIBLY

Special diets for breastfeeding mothers are rarely necessary. They omit valuable foods or put you under pressure to eat foods that you do not like. When you are breastfeeding you need to eat well and you should be able to enjoy your food. A combination of vegetable proteins, whole-grain cereal, fruit, vegetables, and a small amount of animal protein makes the ideal diet. It is a good idea to eat some protein in the morning after you have gone eight to ten hours without food.

You will need to eat regularly throughout the day or you may get hungry. Snacks will help maintain energy: a banana, some grapes or other fruit, a handful of nuts and raisins, a milk drink, a peanut butter, cheese or hummus sandwich, or a bowl of muesli may help you keep your energy level up. If you are concerned about being overweight, keep a bag of fresh finger-sized raw vegetables in the fridge to dip into, and nibble some crunchy crispbread.

In the first three months when you are breastfeeding on demand, it is best, for both your health and the baby's nutrition, that weight loss should take place gradually. If you want to lose weight, delay going on a weight-loss diet until the baby is at least six months old. At that stage it is also a good idea to begin some kind of vigorous physical exercise.

AVOIDING CERTAIN FOODS

Some people may tell you that you should not eat certain foods because they will give the baby colic. All over the world breastfeeding mothers eat foods that in other countries are considered "bad" for the baby. If spices were the cause of colic, the entire infant population of India would be crying nonstop. If garlic contaminated breastmilk and made it wholly unsuitable, babies from many Mediterranean countries would be screaming all the time.

Though it is worth watching to see if any foods you eat affect the baby, most breastfed babies tolerate everything in their mother's diet. If you are aware that you are sensitive to certain foods yourself, your baby may also be uncomfortable after you have eaten these things. Occasionally you might have to do some complicated detective work to discover if a food or food additive is upsetting your baby. Try omitting the suspect food from your diet for a trial week; then reintroduce it gradually and note the result.

HOW MUCH TO DRINK

Breastfeeding mothers used to be advised to drink large quantities of milk, on the grounds that drinking milk would make more milk. This is rather odd reasoning, as cows do not drink milk! They were also told to drink as much fluid as possible. You will probably discover that you want to drink more than usual, and it is a good idea to have a glass of water or juice beside you as you breastfeed. But drinking large quantities of fluid in the evening may make your breasts swollen and uncomfortable by the morning, and forcing yourself to drink excessive quantities ultimately reduces the milk supply.

Advice You Can Ignore

It is often believed that inability to breastfeed is a matter of not having enough milk, and this is why some women can breastfeed and others can't. But it is more subtle than that. Successful breastfeeding has to do with the culture of mothering in which a woman finds herself. The degree of support or discouragement that she receives from those around her, together with her own feelings about breastfeeding, will influence whether she perseveres or gives up. New mothers are targets for much advice about how to feed their babies. A great deal of this advice is untrue.

The dogma that leads to breastfeeding failure goes like this:

"Your nipples are bound to get sore and cracked because you are red-haired/ blonde/have pale skin."

"An older mother should not expect to be able to breastfeed."

"If you have had a cesarean you can't breastfeed."

"If you don't rest you won't be able to breastfeed."

"If you don't put a baby to the breast in the first hour after birth you won't be able to breastfeed."

"Your nipples are too small."

"Your nipples are too flat."

"Your breasts are small so you probably don't have enough breast tissue."

"Big breasts can smother a baby."

"If your mother couldn't breastfeed, you probably can't. It's all a question of genes."

"A baby who cries to be fed more than every three hours isn't getting enough."

"If the baby sucks his fingers after a feed, it shows that you don't have enough milk."

"If you are going back to work you won't be able to breastfeed."

"You can't breastfeed if you're taking drugs for pain relief."

"A baby who has ever been given milk in a bottle refuses the breast because it is easier to suck from a bottle."

"Babies should sleep through the night from four months. If they don't, they can't be getting enough milk."

"Big babies are bound to be hungry, so they need topping up with a bottle."

"Small babies need extra calories, topped up with a bottle."

"If you can't express milk at the end of a feed, the baby must have been sucking on a dry breast."

"A baby should be having solids at four months."

"It's not fair to shut your partner out. A father is closer to his baby if you bottle-feed."

"To treat depression, you must stop breastfeeding. Bottle-feeding is a lot less tiring."

"A child who is breastfed for longer than about 18 months will be overdependent on its mother."

Because people want to help, and are concerned about you or your baby, you may be a target for any of these statements. It helps if you can think, "I've heard this one before." Then you just smile, thank the person for her advice, and continue doing what has felt right for you and your baby all along.

Fountains of Milk

In the first weeks of breastfeeding, your milk may flow copiously and spurt out when your baby feeds, making her choke and splutter and leaving you awash with milk. After about four weeks, however, milk production will settle down and adapt to your baby's needs. It does not mean that you are losing your milk if it is no longer gushing out.

COPING WITH GUSHING MILK

If your milk gushes out, feed from the least full breast first. When the milk ejection reflex begins (see right), it causes milk to flow automatically from both breasts. The full breast will be emptied a bit, making it less over-whelming for the baby if she is put to that side next. It can be difficult for the baby to cope with milk that streams out in great fountains if she is lying flat, so sit her almost upright to feed her.

Feeding may be a messy business to begin with, so have a towel or tissues handy to mop up spills. Wear easily laundered clothing and patterned rather than plain fabrics, so that the milk stains do not show. Cotton is ideal; silk and velvet stain badly. If milk oozes out between feeds, slip paper breast pads inside your bra to absorb the drips. You can also press your elbows firmly against the outer margins of your breasts to reduce the flow.

Though it may be inconvenient, freely flowing milk is a natural safety device against blocked milk ducts, engorgement, stasis (congestion), infection, and breast abscess (see pages 64–66). Women whose milk drips and spurts rarely suffer any of these problems.

COLLECTING EXCESS MILK

You can collect excess milk and store it in the freezer for when you are away from your baby. Or you can give it to a milk bank at your local hospital, where it will be fed to babies in special-care units.

You will need a sterilized bottle, lid, and nipple shield on hand at each feed (see page 136). Before you pick the baby up, place a shield over the breast from which you will not be feeding. When the baby begins to feed, milk will drip and sometimes even pour into the shield. At the end of feeding, tip the milk from the shield into the sterilized bottle, put the lid on, and place it in the fridge right away. You can add more milk to the bottle throughout the day, but after 24 hours it should be put in the freezer, where it will keep for up to six months.

The stimulus from the baby sucking at one breast will start milk flowing in the other breast and you will feel the warmth of the milk ejection reflex in that breast as milk drips out. Keep a towel or tissues handy to cope with leaking milk, or collect the excess milk in a nipple shield and freeze it for later use.

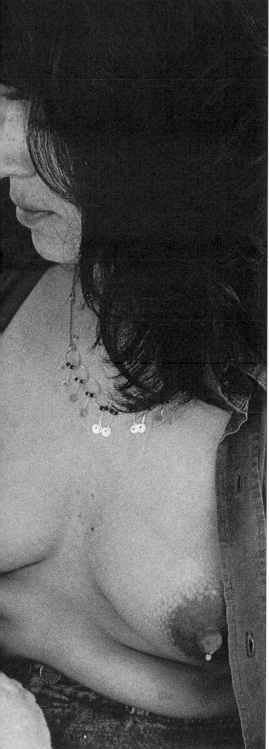

THE MILK EJECTION REFLEX

The hypothalamus sends signals to the pituitary gland to produce hormones.

The pituitary gland produces oxytocin and prolactin that cause the muscle walls of the milk glands to contract.

Milk spurts out when the muscle walls of the milk-producing glands contract.

The baby's sucking stimulates nerve endings in the areola which pass a message to the hypothalamus in the brain.

As your baby latches on, *nerve endings in your breast are stimulated to send a signal to the hypothalamus, a part of the brain that controls metabolism. This in turn signals to the pituitary gland at the base of the brain to release oxytocin and prolactin—the hormones involved in the production and release of milk. Shortly after your baby has begun to suck, these hormones cause the muscle walls of the milk-producing glands to contract, causing the cells lining the glands to squeeze milk into the milk ducts. The milk rushes down the ducts to the nipple and into the baby's mouth. This is known as the milk ejection reflex.*

Milk may pour from your baby's mouth, especially if the flow is sudden and fast (inset, opposite). Breastmilk, unlike infant formula, will not harm the baby if it goes down "the wrong way." It also has healing properties; squirt some over any skin irritation or into a sore eye to soothe it.

If your milk gushes out, your baby may not be able to cope when lying down to nurse. Instead, sit him almost upright on your lap (opposite) and support his back with your arm resting against your raised leg.

After a feed of fast-flowing milk, a baby will need to be held upright (right) while you rub his back to burp him. A baby likes being held on an adult's shoulder so that he can see around him.

The Cream at the Bottom

Breasts are not like milk bottles—the cream is at the bottom, not at the top. The first rush of milk in each breast, known as the foremilk, is thin, and there is a lot of it. The cream, called the hindmilk, comes at the end of the feed as the flow slows down. The baby needs this cream to have a good calorie intake, so it is important to let him suck as long as he likes on the first breast, while he is still hungry enough to get at the creamy milk at the bottom that can be suckled as the breast empties.

THINKING ABOUT WEIGHT GAIN

The old advice about religiously feeding your baby for ten minutes each side may result in your baby getting lashings of thin milk but not enough cream. This means that some babies do not gain weight, and the mother is advised to top up with artificial milk or switch to bottle-feeding, despite a plentiful milk supply.

Sometimes a baby refuses the second breast and screams as if you were offering poison, even though he is obviously still hungry. It might be that he is getting too much dilute foremilk, which will cause gas to form in the intestines. See what happens when you feed him on one side only for as long as he wants. At the next feed, start at the breast on the other side and keep him sucking there.

NO NEED TO CLOCK WATCH

You do not need to time feeds or the length of time between feeds. It is much better to let the baby guide you. There is no rule that babies should go four hours from the start of one feed to the next. Around three hours is common, and very tiny babies may like to feed after two hours.

AVOIDING SORE NIPPLES

It used to be thought that babies made their mothers' nipples sore when they were at the breast for a long time. So midwives and nurses instructed mothers to allow the baby to be at the breast for no longer than ten minutes at each feed. A woman may have only just managed to get her baby fixed firmly on the breast, or a sleepy baby to suck properly, when she was ordered to take the baby off.

Under these conditions, many babies failed to thrive at the breast and were switched to bottle-feeding. Now, however, it is known that sore nipples are almost always the result of poor positioning of the baby at the breast, not of the time spent sucking.

YOU CAN'T OVERFEED

Another reason for timing feeds was the theory that babies might be overfed if allowed to suck their fill. No one has ever been able to produce evidence that a baby can be overfed at the breast. If a baby's tummy is uncomfortably full, he will spit up the excess milk.

A GOOD MILK SUPPLY

If you worry that you are not producing enough milk for your baby, or if other people suggest he ought to be having supplementary milk or solids, here are the signs of a well-fed baby:
• A baby who is obviously gaining weight steadily is getting enough milk.
• A baby who has six or more wet diapers in 24 hours and who is not taking any fluids other than your breastmilk is getting enough milk.
• A baby who has firm muscle tone, bright eyes, and a strong cry and who is lively is certainly getting enough milk.
• A baby who is contented and seems satisfied after feeds is usually getting enough milk.

CAUSES FOR CONCERN

You should be concerned, however, if he shows any of the following signs of dehydration:
• Strong-smelling, bright-yellow urine suggests that he would welcome more fluids. Offer more frequent breastfeeds.
• If the soft spot at the front of the baby's head (the fontanelle) is sunken, he needs milk fast.
• A very dehydrated baby may become sleepy and listless and may seem very "good." He has no energy to cry and isn't getting enough milk.

GROWTH SPURTS

The amount of milk you produce is determined by how often your baby sucks at the breast. When breastfeeding is going well, you will be producing exactly the amount of milk that your baby requires. Babies have growth spurts when they require more milk, usually at five or six weeks, and then again at three and six months. Some babies also have a growth spurt even earlier, at around three weeks. It is quite normal for extra demand for milk to accompany a growth spurt.

INCREASING YOUR SUPPLY

To pep up the milk supply, feed more often. My 24-Hour Peak Production Plan (see page 106) entails feeding every two to three hours. The stimulation of the baby's more frequent sucking works wonders. Let your baby decide when he has had enough at the first breast, and encourage him to go on as long as he likes. Then put him to the other side.

Repeat this throughout the day. If he sleeps longer between feeds at night, take the chance to get some sleep yourself and wait to offer the breast until he wakes. Your supply will usually catch up with the increased demand in 24 hours, though occasionally a mother has to feed her baby this frequently for 48 hours before she has an abundant supply of milk.

Ensure that your baby is in a good position and latched on well at each feed. If he is not milking the breast and drawing down hindmilk, every time, you will not produce more.

WHAT CAUSES REDUCTION IN SUPPLY

Some kinds of medication may decrease your milk supply, at least temporarily. These include laxatives, diuretics, contraceptive pills, and antibiotics. Your doctor may not have realized you were breastfeeding when this drug was prescribed. Alternative forms of drugs that do not affect the supply of milk are usually available, so discuss this with your doctor. The list on pages 69–71 may help you.

A baby who is ill or under the weather may suck weakly and sleep a great deal. Even a stuffy nose or a slight fever may result in your baby's sleeping much more than usual. It is best to follow the baby's lead for feeding. You cannot force-feed a baby. But when feeds are less frequent, the supply of breastmilk is temporarily reduced. You can stimulate your breasts by expressing milk instead (see page 136).

A satisfied baby often falls asleep at the breast, lips slightly parted, and smiling occasionally, as if he is having a happy dream.

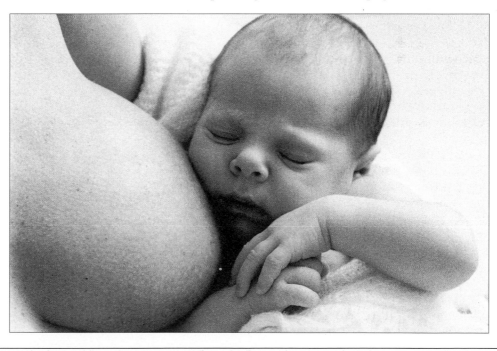

When a Baby Has Had Enough

You may wonder how you can tell when your baby has had enough milk and it is time either to switch to the other side or to draw the feed to a close. For some women this is a real worry. In some ways it would make it so much easier if we had transparent, plastic breasts, so that we could watch the milk level going down notch by notch, and know that the baby was drinking a certain amount. But it would be nowhere near as comfortable or loving. You would not be able to enjoy such long cuddles, and the baby would not receive the same warmth and softness from the contact with your body.

THE SATISFIED BABY

Babies are not like cars that you fill up with gas—they do not require the same amount of milk at each feed. Babies have their own internal appetite regulators, and usually stop vigorous sucking when they have had enough. As a feed draws to a close, the rate of swallowing to sucking slows down. The baby likes to suck but cannot be bothered to swallow because she is feeling satisfied and contented. Her eyes close, her head feels heavy, and her limbs are relaxed and floppy. Her breathing slows down, too—the excited breathing of anticipating a feed and of the early thrilling gulps is replaced by a much gentler tempo. Gradually she falls asleep, still latched on firmly to the breast.

THE BREAST AS COMFORT

The problem is that as the baby drifts off to sleep, she may be suddenly jolted awake by being moved, by some internal happening, such as a bowel movement, or by an external noise. Then she discovers she isn't at the breast and starts frantically searching for it. You offer it, she latches on, gives a few sucks, and then falls asleep again. Clearly, she is using the breast for comfort. There is nothing wrong with it, though it may be inconvenient for you. Babies usually enjoy sucking so much that they suck willingly whenever and wherever they are offered the breast: even if they are tired out and really just want a chance to sleep; even if their tummies are full almost to overflowing; even if they have dirtied their diapers and would really like to be changed. Sucking is a baby's main way of receiving comfort from the mother.

PLAYING AT THE BREAST

1 The baby's rate of swallowing to sucking slows down (above) and she starts to play. She licks the nipple, pats or strokes the breast, and discovers her own foot.

2 She looks around (top opposite), attracted by a sudden sound or movement, or by a change in the light, and is fascinated by the things people are doing. She absorbs everything she can hear, see, and feel.

3 She slips off the breast (bottom opposite) and starts enjoying her hands instead, or finds a piece of fabric to suck. She is relaxed and may smile, coo, and gurgle.

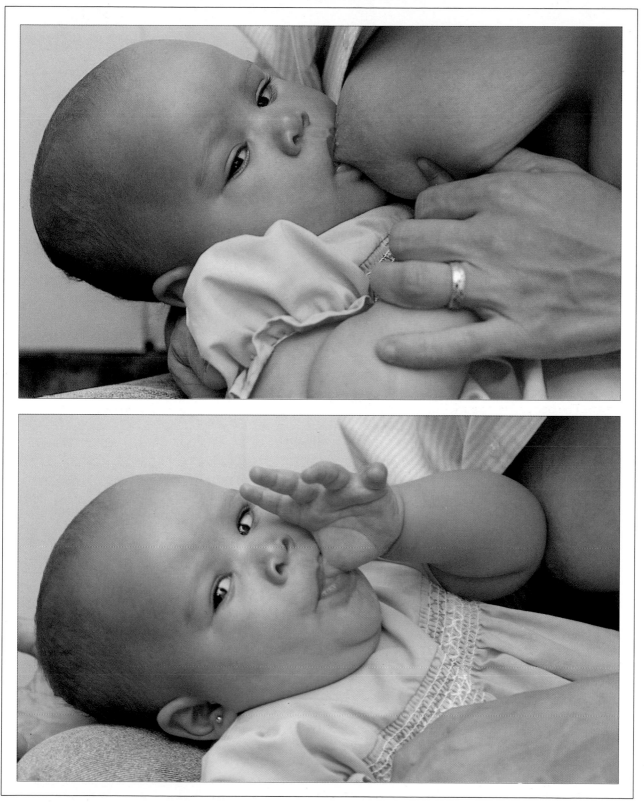

OTHER FORMS OF COMFORT

Breastfeeding is the most loving and effective way of giving comfort to a young baby. Yet as the baby grows you can show her that there are other good ways of being comforted: simply being held, stroked or patted, or hearing your voice or the voice of someone else she knows well. If you are sensitive to your baby's responses, you will know when you can provide other forms of comfort. Until that time is reached—often during the baby's second month of life—the breast is the surest remedy for a baby's distress. Offering that comfort readily and freely does not mean you will condition her to having the nipple constantly in her mouth.

PLAYING WITH THE NIPPLE

When a baby is not hungry but is luxuriating in the sweetness of the breast, she may play with and nibble the nipple. She purses her lips and pushes the nipple from the back of her mouth so that she is just getting the odd drip of milk—not the full flood that comes when she uses her jaw to pump milk. Interspersed with nipple nibbling, her mouth makes little twitching, smiling movements. She sucks again vigorously for a few seconds as if to tell you she is still busily occupied. But you know, and the baby knows, that the feed has finished.

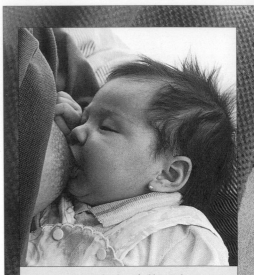

When your baby falls asleep at the breast, her body soft and loose, her head heavy, her eyes closed, and milk still in her mouth, you will have no doubt she has had enough and you will feel satisfied together.

SUCKING AT ONE BREAST

Sometimes one breastful of milk is enough. A woman with a physical disability or who has a one-sided mastectomy can breastfeed at one side only. But for all women, it is much better for the baby to continue at one breast until she indicates by her behavior that she has had enough, than to take her off and move her over to the other side because you believe you must use both breasts at each feed. If you constantly switch your baby from one breast to the other, the baby will get a large amount of thin foremilk, but her hunger may never be satisfied. Foremilk is high in lactose. A baby who takes in too much lactose cannot break down and digest this form of sugar. Instead, intestinal gas is produced, which leads to a distended stomach, pockets of bubbles in the large bowel, pain, jet-propelled bowel movements that are often flecked with green, and long bouts of distressed crying.

RELIEVING A FULL BREAST

If you are left after a feed with one breast well used and the other feeling as if it will pop because it is so full, put a hot facecloth on the overloaded breast or squeeze warm water on it and lean over a sink to let excess milk flow out. Or you can express and store the milk (see page 136).

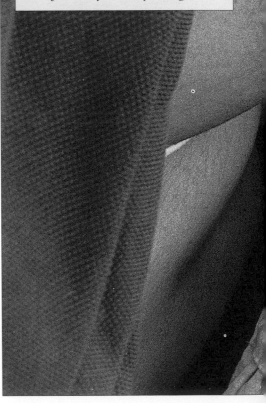

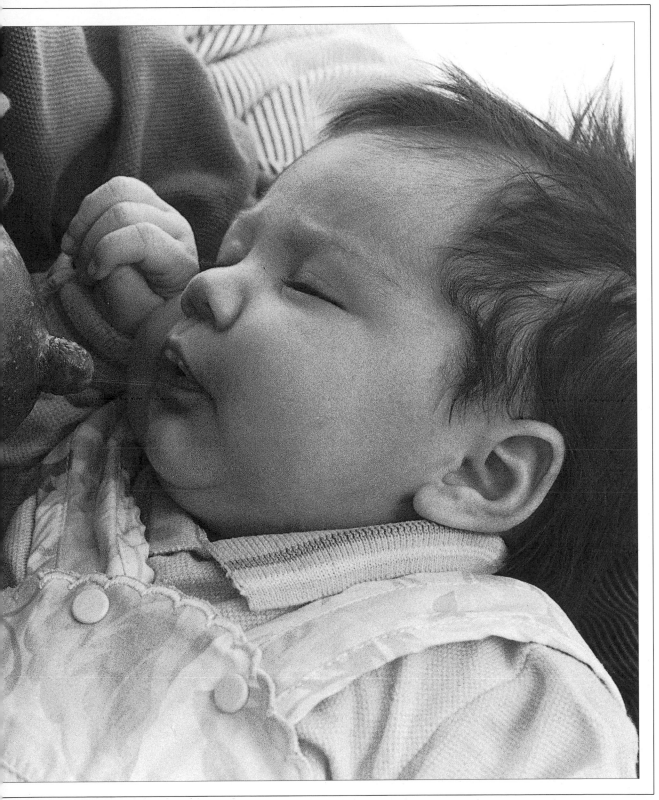

FORESEEING PROBLEMS

Sore and Cracked Nipples

SORE NIPPLES CAN DEVELOP CRACKS if not treated early. Cracked nipples can be agony. The main cause is poor positioning of the baby at the breast. A baby who is not latched on correctly tends to chew on the nipple stem in an attempt to obtain milk (see pages 30–39).

Sometimes only one nipple is sore. This is because it is simpler to latch the baby on to one breast than the other, depending on whether you are left- or right-handed. So try a different position: hold her under your right arm, with her feet pointing behind. Cradle her head in your hand and let your breast drop into her mouth (see pages 28–29).

Another cause of sore nipples is using soap, creams, and lotions to which you are sensitive. Antiseptics, lanolin-based creams, and bubble baths may cause or exacerbate the damage.

MOUTH INFECTION

A yeast infection in your baby's mouth can also result in nipple soreness. Candida (thrush) consists of small white patches in the mouth that cannot be shifted when you touch them with your finger. The baby's mouth gets sore, as well as your nipple, and you continue to reinfect each other unless you are both treated.

You can apply the medication prescribed by your doctor to your baby's mouth immediately before a feed, so that when the baby latches on to the breast your nipples receive the benefit as well. You can help your body cure candida by omitting yeast and sugar from your diet.

TREATING SORE NIPPLES

Always offer your baby the least tender breast first. It will also help if you feed your baby before she is desperately hungry, so that her sucking is less vigorous. Allow her to suck her fill on the first breast before putting her on the other. If she has sucked well at the first breast,

she may need very little from the other side, or not want it at all, so that the tender nipple can rest and recover.

Sore nipples heal in the air, so if you get the chance to walk around topless, this will help. Sleep naked, and lie on a towel to soak up leaking milk. Avoid using plastic-lined bra pads, as they make the nipples soggy and may lead to infection. Allow air to circulate around your nipples.

MOIST WOUND HEALING

For a long time the theory about healing sore nipples has been that they must be kept dry. Yet with other wounds and skin cracks dermatologists usually advise moist healing. They aim to increase the moisture content of the skin with a cream, that serves as a barrier that slows down evaporation of moisture naturally present in the skin and prevents further drying and cracking. The same principle applies to sore nipples.*

Some women find that smoothing a little breastmilk over the tender area at the end of a feed helps healing. Others prefer an over-the-counter cream. Experiment to find out what is right for you, bearing in mind that it is possible to have an allergic reaction to creams and oils. Avoid vitamin E oil, or use it sparingly, since vitamin E may be stored in the baby's liver and accumulate over time.*

WHITE NIPPLE

Sometimes a woman has sore nipples that go white and are either numb or burn and tingle. This is often the result of poor positioning of the baby. Ask someone experienced to help you get the baby well latched on.

White nipple may also be caused by getting cold or by emotional stress. Smoking and coffee make the condition worse. Taking evening primrose oil—up to 1,000 mg every day—may help in the long run.*

Sore nipples heal quickly in the air, so it helps to go topless or without a bra whenever possible to let air circulate around your nipples.

Engorgement and Mastitis

Breasts that are engorged with milk are sometimes so distended that the nipples retreat under surrounding tissue. They feel like hot bricks, and are extremely painful to touch. If not treated rapidly, engorgement will lead to mastitis, which is congestion of the milk ducts and inflammation of the breast.

WHAT CAUSES ENGORGEMENT?
Engorgement is preventable. It is caused either by imposing long intervals between feeds—especially overnight—so that the breasts are not sufficiently milked, or by bad positioning of the baby at the breast so that milk is not adequately drained from the lactiferous sinuses. If you are a copious milk producer, even one hurried feed in which the baby has not been well positioned,

or one unusually long interval between feeds because your baby is sleeping extra soundly, may lead to engorgement.

To prevent your breasts from becoming engorged when you are apart from your baby at any time, express some milk as soon as you feel full (see pages 136–39). Express just enough to make you feel comfortable, or it will stimulate production of yet more milk

TREATING ENGORGEMENT
To treat engorged breasts, sit in a hot bath or under a shower and express enough milk to make you feel comfortable again. Directing a hand-held spray of hot water on the breasts brings relief. Once you are more comfortable, put the baby to the breast and let her feed.

AN ENGORGED BREAST
The hard, distended breast prevents the baby from taking a good mouthful of areola and nipple. She can only achieve a poor latch that leaves her sucking at the nipple instead of the breast. Latched on like this she will not have a good feed (see page 33). In any case, the breast's swollen milk glands compress the milk ducts and reduce the flow of milk, further preventing her from feeding well. You can get into a vicious cycle where the milk ducts cannot be drained because of engorgement, but until they are drained, you will remain engorged.

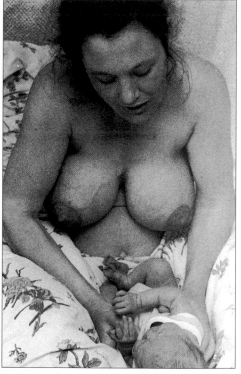

Engorged breasts are swollen, hot and tender. The milk-producing glands feel hard and lumpy, often under the arms.

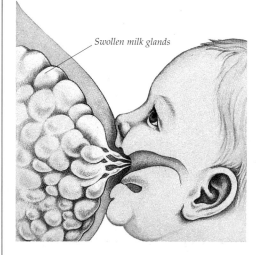

Swollen milk glands

While your baby becomes frustrated, your breasts and nipples become sore. It is important to understand the signs and effects of engorgement as it can turn feeding into a struggle for both you and your baby. It may also lead to blocked ducts and very painful mastitis.

Expressing milk by hand will help to relieve an engorged breast. Lean over a sink to allow the milk to drip out, and gently massage the breast to encourage the milk to flow.

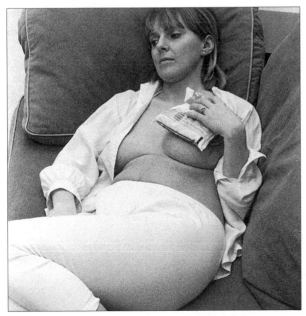

A packet of frozen peas or a bag of ice cubes rested against a hot, engorged breast can feel very comforting and bring immediate relief.

An engorged breast needs to be handled with great care. The swollen glands can easily be bruised. In some hospitals, nurses offer massage to treat engorged breasts. If you need to massage your breasts to get a milk ejection reflex (see page 53), it is safer for you to massage them yourself than for a nurse to do it.

WHAT IS MASTITIS?

Mastitis is inflammation of the breast, with or without infection. The first line of treatment should not be antibiotics. At least half of all women with mastitis do not have an infection.* A red patch that is tender to the touch appears, often in the lower part of the right breast, and you develop a headache and run a temperature of 100°F or more. You feel feverish, tired, and achy.

The cause of mastitis is a blockage of milk in the ducts deep in the breast. It often occurs in the right breast in right-handed women, because it is slightly more difficult to latch the baby on to the breast using the left hand. And it occurs more in the lower part because when you sit hunched up, this part of the breast is trapped against your body, and milk is not emptied from it. Wearing a bra that is too tight and that clasps the lower part of the breast against your body, or always holding the baby tensely with your elbows firmly pressing against your breast, can have the same effect of trapping milk.

TREATING MASTITIS

The best way to treat mastitis is exactly the same as the best way to avoid it: ensure that the baby is correctly latched on so that she can milk the breast thoroughly.

If a red patch develops, ensure that the baby's lower jaw clasps the part of the breast over the spot where the inflammation has appeared. You can probably do this more easily if you tuck the baby's body under your arm with her feet pointing behind you, and cup her head in your hand to guide her into the right position (see page 26). Or lie on your side with the baby lying alongside. Put the baby to the inflamed breast first. Lift your breast as you fix the baby on, so that the lower part is not pressing against your ribcage.

Feed as much as you can on the inflamed side, the aim being to "strip" the breast of all the milk available. Some women use a breast pump to help them achieve this. The milk is perfectly safe for your baby, so do not throw it away— freeze it for future use. A well-used breast does not get mastitis, so make sure that your breast is used thoroughly. Before the baby comes to the breast, and during intervals in sucking, massage the sore part by pressing and squeezing it with your fingers deep in the glandular tissue. This will help free the milk.

EASING THE DISCOMFORT

For your comfort, you can sponge your breast with warm water. Have frequent baths or showers, and either direct a spray of hot water on your breast or kneel in the bath so that your breasts are suspended in the warm water.

When you are lying down or sitting and relaxing, you can rest a hot compress against the red patch. Or you may prefer a cold one, the simplest and easiest being a small bag of frozen peas or ice cubes wrapped in a small towel, diapers, or facecloth.

Do not forget your other breast while you are doing this. If the baby is not using the second breast as much, apply hot compresses and express milk to keep it flowing.

Any exercise that entails hitting a ball with an over-arm movement, such as tennis or badminton, increases blood circulation to the inflamed area and aids healing. Vigorous arm movements of the kind used in washing and wringing out diapers by hand, washing a floor, or cleaning a window will also help—something you may not usually want to do!

This does not mean that you should take on all the housework. You will benefit from as much sleep as you can get. You can take Tylenol every four hours to treat the headache, and take your temperature every four hours or so, too. If mastitis is being relieved, your temperature will go down over a period of 48 hours, until it is normal again. But you will start to feel better, and the breast will feel softer, long before this. If, after a couple of days, you find self-treatment ineffective, see your doctor.

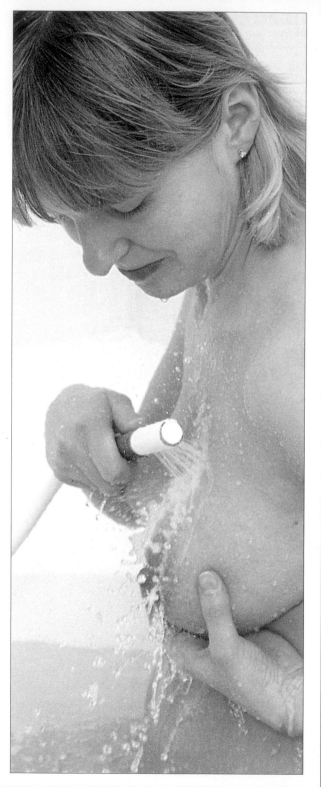

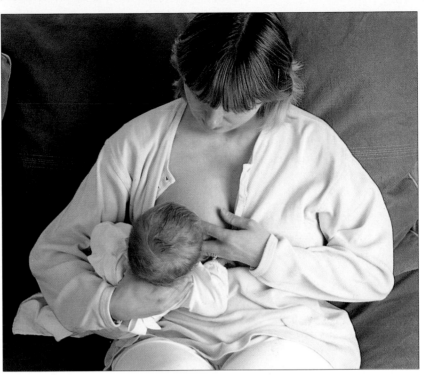

Directing a hand-held ***shower spray*** *of hot water on to your breasts (opposite) will help milk to spurt out, relieving engorgement.*

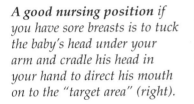

A ***good nursing position*** *if you have sore breasts is to tuck the baby's head under your arm and cradle his head in your hand to direct his mouth on to the "target area" (right).*

Getting Enough Sleep

Newborn babies do not know the difference between day and night, so they may want frequent feeding at nighttime and sleep solidly in the morning or afternoon. Don't try to keep going during the day; take every opportunity to rest.

The time to catch up on extra sleep is right after your baby has fed. If you do urgent work first, you may never get the chance. Look at your baby's sleep patterns and discover a time when she takes a longish nap. If you have older children, relax by setting aside a regular quiet time with them, when you can read a story, sing nursery rhymes, or do something peaceful like making cut-out dolls from a newspaper. Keep special playthings for this time. The children will look forward to it as a space in the day when they have your full attention.

A new baby makes a lot of work. If there is a chance of getting help with chores, grab it. It is more important that you get enough sleep than that you catch up with other work.

Many babies cry in the evening and need constant attention. But you may be lucky and have one who sleeps during the evening. If so, arrange for your partner to take over for a few hours so that you can sleep. If you have expressed milk into a bottle or have stored some in the refrigerator, your partner can give a bottle of breastmilk if the baby needs it.

FEEDING AT NIGHT

If you feel exhausted, but your baby does not drop off to sleep after a night feed, your partner can take her to a different room to settle her down. Then they can both creep back in, or bed down elsewhere, to make sure that you get a spell of uninterrupted sleep. If you express milk, someone else may be able to feed the baby with a bottle of your milk at night. Though she may only sleep for an hour or so longer, and then want you—and only you—that extra time can give you some much-needed rest.

If You Are Ill

If you are ill while you are breastfeeding, it is better if you arrange for someone else to do the housework than for you to give up breastfeeding or hand over the care of the baby. Yet you will probably be advised by those concerned about you to give up breastfeeding because they feel that it must be exhausting you. In reality, breastfeeding can make life easier for you. You do not have to spend time sterilizing bottles and making up artificial feeds. Instead, you and the baby can cuddle up in bed and enjoy each other. Knowing you can offer your milk increases your self-esteem and confidence as a mother at a time when you may be especially anxious.

The rush of prolactin and other hormones in a woman's bloodstream while she is breastfeeding sometimes results in remission of symptoms of chronic illness. This applies particularly to diabetic mothers and those suffering from arthritis, lupus, and, possibly, multiple sclerosis.

If you are diabetic, you may wonder whether your milk is safe for your baby. It is. Studies show that breastfeeding helps protect a baby against diabetes, too.*

GOING TO THE HOSPITAL

If you have to go to the hospital, you should be able to take your baby in with you so that you can feed him. If you have a general anesthetic, the drug will pass into your milk, so the baby may need to be given either your own or another mother's expressed milk in a bottle for 12 to 24 hours. On the other hand, some modern anesthetics pass through your system very quickly, and you can breastfeed as soon as you are awake. Discuss this with your anesthetist in advance. When you are feeling weak or drowsy, make sure that someone else is present to lift and change the baby for you.

RELACTATING

If you lose your milk when you are ill, you may decide you want to relactate. Your milk will return, but it will take up to ten days. You need to organize practical help so that you can lie in bed with your baby, letting him suck as much as he wants. This sucking is the most effective way of producing milk.

Empty your breasts with an electric pump four or five times a day after the baby has suckled. You can express this milk straight into a bottle and give it to him. At first you will only produce a few drops, but that is still a triumph. Bottle-feed the baby after she has had some time at the breast, but gradually reduce this as you feel your own milk return.

TAKING DRUGS WHEN BREASTFEEDING

Try to avoid taking drugs when you are breastfeeding. This applies to over-the-counter and recreational drugs as well as prescribed medicines. Almost all drugs enter breastmilk, but usually in amounts so low that the baby is not affected. According to an expert who is both a pediatrician and a pharmacologist, the concentration of a drug in milk depends on: 1) its solubility, 2) the size of the molecules, 3) the amount that gets into your blood, 4) whether it binds with your blood proteins, 5) the drug's half-life in your blood and the baby's blood. (The half-life of a drug is the time it takes for the concentration to be reduced by one half.)* Drugs that affect the central nervous system are the ones that most easily enter milk and that reach the highest concentrations.

In their product leaflets pharmaceutical companies warn against breastfeeding mainly to protect themselves against any possible litigation, but if you have to take medicine, there are usually drugs available that have little or no effect on the baby. With commonly prescribed psychotropic drugs, such as tranquilizers, sedatives, and antihistamines, the usual effect is to make a baby drowsy. A drowsy baby won't suck vigorously, so breastfeeding is more difficult and the volume of milk is reduced. The information about the psychotropic drugs in the list opposite is based on advice from a Professor of Perinatal Psychiatry.*

Drugs and Breastfeeding

The following is a list of just some of the prescribed, recreational, and over-the-counter drugs that a woman may consider taking.* If you are prescribed any medicine, remind your doctor that you are breastfeeding. Be sure to mention any drugs you may already be taking as some drugs interact with others.

Acyclovir ointment Used for herpes, this preparation is unlikely to be harmful. But if you put it on your nipples, wash if off before breastfeeding.

Alcohol This enters breastmilk in large amounts. It can make the baby sleepy and decrease your milk supply. If you want to have an alcoholic drink, do so immediately after a breastfeed.

Antibiotics Generally, most antibiotics from the penicillin and cephalosporin groups are safe to take while breastfeeding. However, they may make a baby thirsty and cause diarrhea. Very little *tetracycline* enters breastmilk and it is approved by the American Academy of Pediatrics. *Minocycline* may be absorbed more readily, but short-term treatment is unlikely to harm a baby. *Chloramphenicol* is best avoided, as is *metronidazole* (Flagyl) and *nalidixic acid*.

Anticoagulants Most anticoagulants are not dangerous. *Warfarin* is passed into milk, but in small amounts. Watch the baby for bruising and bleeding. *Heparin* does not enter the milk.

Antidepressants These often have surprisingly little effect on babies. A baby receives five percent or less of the mother's dose. The exceptions are the tricyclic antidepressants (e.g. Elavil, Pamelor). *Lithium*, too, passes easily into breastmilk, and even though the dose the baby gets is small, it may affect the thyroid gland. If the baby's electrolyte balance is disturbed by a bout of diarrhea and vomiting, this dose could be toxic. *Fluoxetine* (Prozac) passes into the milk in small

amounts, but has a long half-life, so in theory it can accumulate in the baby. If the baby becomes irritable, switch to *sertraline* (Zoloft).

Antifungal drugs *Nystatin*, used to treat candida, or thrush, is unlikely to be secreted in milk.

Antihistamines *Chloropheniramine* (Chlorotab, Phenetron) and *Dyphenhydramine* (Benadryl, Nordryl) have little effect.

Antihypertensives These are used to treat high blood pressure. *Methyldopa* is not harmful to breastfed babies and very little *minoxidil* is transferred in breastmilk, though long-term exposure should be avoided. Babies are highly sensitive to ACE inhibitors, which are used to dilate blood vessels. If you take them, watch for signs of floppiness in the baby's limbs and have the baby's blood pressure checked. Beta-blockers seem to be safer. *Propranolol* probably carries least risk; less than 0.1 percent of the mother's dose passes to the baby. Of the calcium channel blockers (also used to help dilate blood vessels), the American Academy of Pediatrics recommends *diltiazem* or *nifedipine* for breastfeeding mothers.

Asthma drugs *Epinephrine* (Nephron) and *Cromolyn sodium* (Intal) are safe. There **are no** reports of harm to the baby from mothers using inhalers (Ventolin, Bronkaid). **See also Steroids.**

Caffeine Little *caffeine* enters breastmilk. If a mother drinks more than six cups a day, however, a newborn may become irritable.

Cannabis (marijuana) Levels of *cannabis* in breastmilk are eight times higher than in the mother's blood. This can make the baby drowsy.

Cocaine *Cocaine* can be absorbed by a baby through breastmilk or through inhaling the smoke. It may make him very jumpy. It is especially dangerous to put cocaine on nipples.

Contraceptive pill Birth control pills may reduce your milk supply when you first take them. Wait until breastfeeding is going well before you go on the Pill, then feed more frequently to build up the supply again. The combined estrogen-progestogen pill should not be taken.

Cough medicines Iodine appears in some cough medicines and can lead to thyroid depression in the baby. *Guaifenesin* is better.

Drugs for epilepsy *Phenytoin* is safe; even though 50 percent of the drug in the mother's circulation passes into the breastmilk, the baby is able to excrete it readily. *Carbamazepine* passes into breastmilk in a higher concentration—about 60 percent—but does not seem to harm the baby. *Ethosuximide* is approved by the American Academy of Pediatrics for use by breastfeeding mothers.

Diuretics Used to treat high blood pressure and heart, kidney, and liver conditions, these should not be taken as they reduce the milk supply.

Hepatitis B vaccine There have been no reports of harmful effects.

Herbal remedies and teas Ointments and poultices of *comfrey* should not be used by a breastfeeding mother. Never take herb teas unless you know what is in them. Avoid Chinese teas, and also avoid *comfrey, germander, mistletoe, margosa oil, maté tea, skullcap,* and *pennyroyal.* They can cause liver damage.

Heroin This drug enters the breastmilk and can kill your baby.

Hexachlorophene This antiseptic is transferred to milk through the skin. Avoid.

Insulin Used to treat diabetes, *insulin* is not secreted into milk.

Iopamidol This is a radiocontrast agent that contains *iodine,* but it does not pass into the blood, and is unlikely to enter breastmilk.

Laxatives The type that adds bulk to feces is not absorbed from your intestinal tract. They are less harmful for the baby than aperients, which make your bowels work faster and may make the baby's stools loose.

Malaria drugs Small amounts enter the milk and are not dangerous. However, watch in case the baby becomes jumpy.

Methadone Approved by the American Academy of Pediatrics for breastfeeding women, the dose of *methadone* should be less than 20 mg in 24 hours.

Methylergonovine (Methergine) This is used to treat heavy bleeding after birth and is safer than *ergonovine,* which reduces the milk supply. Only a trace of *Methergine* enters the milk.

Methotrexate Used to treat arthritis and cancer, *methotrexate* is dangerous for your baby.

Migraine drugs These may not cause a problem if used short term, but in high doses and over time they are toxic for babies. *Ergotamine* (Cafergot) is not recommended. It inhibits prolactin, reducing production of breastmilk. *Sumatriptan* (Imitrex) is a newer vasoconstrictor. Little enters breastmilk, and only a tiny amount is absorbed in the baby's mouth.

Nicotine The nicotine from cigarettes passes into breastmilk easily and reduces milk production. It is also very harmful for the baby, causing vomiting, loose stools, rapid heartbeat and jumpiness. It may be one factor in Sudden Infant Death Syndrome (crib death). Nicotine patches are a little less dangerous than nicotine from cigarettes.

Painkillers Though it is usually safe to take *aspirin* in low doses, extremely large amounts can produce slight bleeding in the baby and *aspirin* is also implicated in the development of Reye's Syndrome. Use *ibuprofen* or *acetaminophen* (Tylenol) instead. *Acetaminophen* in normal doses is safe during breastfeeding since the baby gets less than one percent of the mother's dose. *Morphine* enters the milk in very small amounts and is not readily absorbed by the baby's mouth. But if it is taken along with other drugs, watch for possible harmful effects on the baby. It is best not to use *codeine* in the first two weeks of the baby's life, because small amounts enter breastmilk, but after that time low doses of *codeine* have little or no effect on the baby. *Piroxicam* and *naproxen*, for arthritis, are approved by the American Academy of Pediatrics. *Demerol* is secreted in breastmilk and builds up in a baby's blood. It makes him sleepy and interferes with breastfeeding.

Radioactive iodine Used as a tracer, radioactive iodine is present in breastmilk for up to 96 hours. Express as much milk as you can in advance and store it in the refrigerator or freezer, or arrange for a friend to breastfeed for you. During the tests, express and throw away milk, and continue this for 16 days after tests are completed.

Radiopaque agents These are used to see organs during X rays and scans. Though radiopaque agents contain iodine, they do not enter breastmilk.

Rubella vaccination This is usually advised after childbirth for women who are not immune to rubella. But it should be avoided if a baby is premature, because the vaccine is transmitted in milk and could infect a vulnerable baby.

Sedatives and hypnotics These should not be taken for more than a couple of weeks because you can become dependent on them. It is probably wise to express and throw away milk until you have stopped taking them.

Steroids Steroids taken via an inhaler do not affect the baby. A woman who is prescribed steroid pills to treat asthma, rheumatoid arthritis, or cancer is usually advised not to breastfeed. Systemic steroids, taken by mouth, pass into the bloodstream and into your milk. If you are prescribed systemic steroids for a period of not longer than ten days, express and freeze milk before taking the first dose. *Prednisone* is safe in low doses.

Tamoxifen A woman taking this anticancer drug should not breastfeed.

Thyroid drugs For overactive thyroid, *propylthiouracil* passes into breastmilk in small amounts and the baby will need monitoring. For underactive thyroid, *thyroxine* and *liothyronine* are both safe for breastfeeding mothers, provided the baby is monitored.

Tranquilizers These may sedate a baby and a sleepy baby does not suck vigorously. *Diazepam* (Valium) may make a baby drowsy and floppy. It is best to avoid it in the first weeks, as it can build up and cause reduced muscle tone in the baby. An older baby gets rid of Valium more efficiently. *Oxazepam* is an alternative; the baby gets less that one-thousandth of the mother's dose. *Meprobomate* is an older anti-anxiety drug; two to four times as much passes into milk as into the mother's blood, so it should be avoided. Take special care if you take a very strong tranquilizer, such as *chlorpromazine* or *haloperidol*. But the benefits of breastfeeding probably outweigh risks, unless you are very ill and your doses are at the top of the recommended range. Then it may be wise to stop breastfeeding, at least while you continue to take these drugs.

Vitamins Vitamin A is fat-soluble, so large amounts enter breastmilk and build up in the baby's liver. There is no need to take vitamin A supplements, as breastmilk is rich in this vitamin. Do not take more than the prescribed doses of vitamin B3 (*nicotinic acid, niacin*), as it can damage a baby's liver. Vitamin B6 (*pyridoxamine*) in high doses reduces production of breastmilk. Do not take more than 25 mg a day. Vitamin B12 is a useful supplementary vitamin for vegan mothers, who may be short of it. Stick to the recommended dose of vitamin D or it may raise the baby's calcium levels too high. Vitamin E is secreted in the milk in higher concentrations than its levels in your blood and is stored in the baby's liver. Depending on the vitamin E preparation (commonly *DL-alpha tocopherol acetate*), do not exceed 16 mg a day. If you use vitamin E cream on sore nipples, apply it sparingly and infrequently.

Thinking of Giving Up?

Many women give up breastfeeding at six to eight weeks. Others struggle on for three months, getting more and more miserable, and then give up. It is usually because they are not producing enough milk, the baby is failing to gain weight and is crying, and days and nights have merged to become one long 24-hour endurance test. The mother is exhausted and on the verge of tears and everyone else is worried. Bottle-feeding seems to be the only answer. But it isn't. There are several reasons for a crisis at six to eight weeks.

UNSATISFIED BABY

A baby who has done well up to now may have a growth spurt and always seem hungry, asking to be fed every hour or so (see page 57). To make more milk a mother needs to breastfeed more frequently, ensuring that at four or five of these hourly feeds the baby empties the breast, as much as possible. If the baby does not do this, the mother can express any milk that remains, using a pump (see pages 138–39), to give to the baby later.

REDUCED MILK SUPPLY

A woman who started off with a copious milk supply but who has not learned how to get the baby latched on is now faced with a reduced supply. When milk is plentiful, foremilk pours into the baby's mouth, and she may have to do little but lie with an open mouth, exerting occasional pressure with her lips to keep it flowing. This means that the breast is never thoroughly milked and the supply is reduced. The way to get a good supply is to learn how to achieve a firm latch (see pages 30–39).

POOR WEIGHT GAIN

If a baby's weight gain is not steady, doctors and healthcare providers are concerned that feeding should be well established in one form or another by now, and may put pressure on a mother to opt for bottle-feeding. When there have been problems with breastfeeding from the beginning, the woman is often not quite out of

the woods by six weeks and is anxious that she may harm her baby by continuing to breastfeed. But if she feels that breastfeeding is getting easier, it is worth resisting the pressure to bottle-feed.

UNCOMFORTABLE POSITION

A baby who has grown fast is no longer able to latch on well in a position that was fine when she was smaller. A big baby is best held either lying right across your body, her tummy against your tummy, with your hand on the opposite side supporting her head, or sitting or standing between your legs so that she is virtually upright. This is the time to explore some new positions.

SORE NIPPLES OR BREASTS

A woman with sore and bleeding nipples or breasts with hard red lumps may decide she can no longer tolerate the pain. Nipples that are damaged like this are almost invariably the result of not getting a good latch. Sore breasts may be caused by engorgement and mastitis (see pages 64–66).

COMPARISON WITH BOTTLE-FEEDING

When a mother meets other mothers and babies she may see that bottle-fed babies are more placid, go longer between feeds, and that their weight gain is good. She naturally wants the best for her baby, so she switches to the bottle.

Breastmilk is more quickly digested than cow's milk and is absorbed completely, so the baby is ready for another feed sooner. A bottle-fed baby may put on weight faster, because cow's milk is for calves, not babies, and they grow faster. There is no evidence that this is beneficial.

FEELINGS OF INADEQUACY

At about six weeks a new mother and those around her may feel that she should be "back to normal." Bottle-feeding may seem the only solution to chaos. For many women, breastfeeding is lonely, and they need all the support and encouragement they can get.

"I admire what she's done for our baby. She found breastfeeding very demanding but kept right on. Sam has had none of the colds other children have had and is always happy."

GETTING TO KNOW YOUR BABY

"I Am Your Mother"

WHEN A WOMAN BREASTFEEDS she usually scans her baby's face, looking with great intensity at eyes, nose, mouth, ears, the intricate whorls of the hair and the different planes of the face. She looks for any sign from the baby that he recognizes her.

THE BABY'S WORLD

You may be disappointed in the early weeks to discover that your baby looks right through you and concentrates on something over your shoulder. It can seem as if he is not interested in you, and even rejects you. He is engrossed in the interplay of light and shade and the complex texture of fabrics and tiny patterns. The baby does not just wait for objects to come within his range of vision. He searches actively for things on which to focus.

Every now and again he may, as if by chance, gaze at your smiling mouth and your shining eyes. But he does not know at first exactly where to find them. When you are feeding him he may stare at the curve of your breast, or at a pattern on your clothing. All the time you long for him to look you in the eyes and acknowledge you.

FOCUSING RANGE

The newborn baby can focus on objects that are no closer than eight or nine inches and no farther away than eighteen inches, so he sees best when your face is somewhere in this range. When you are breastfeeding, your baby is at just the right distance to focus on your face; soon after the first few weeks, his eyes will invariably seek yours, and you will feel that instead of a little groping, sucking animal, your baby is a person, and that he knows you.

A MOTHER'S INSTINCTS

If you are not rushed, or under other pressures that prevent you from trusting your intuitive feelings, you can adapt to your baby's needs with sensitive understanding. You pick up your baby because you realize that he wants to be held upright, or to lie against your body where he can hear the reassuring beat of your heart and your breathing, or to feel your warmth and breathe in your special smell. Or you change his position so that he can see what is going on around him, because you know that he needs stimulation from colors, shapes, and sounds.

RESPONDING TO YOUR BABY

You do these things casually, only half thinking, often with your mind on other matters. Yet you are absolutely right in responding to your baby's needs in this way. And if an action is not right, you know it immediately, and spontaneously adapt what you are doing until the baby tells you that he is bored and restless and wants something else, or that he is hungry and wants the breast again.

UNDERSTANDING YOUR BABY

When your baby starts to cry in a different way, you understand that he does not want any more of this. You may try moving him a little, but he is still restless. You hold him and it's still clear from his nuzzling and rooting that he seeks the breast avidly, so you put down whatever you are doing and respond immediately. Or perhaps he snuffles around halfheartedly but is easily distracted, and you know that he would like the breast again, but can wait until he is really hungry.

A mother can interpret immediately the cry that tells her that her baby is frantic for a feed. She may not be able to analyze exactly how she knows, but she is quite certain. She feels in herself the baby's panic, but it is important that she does not let it overwhelm her. She responds in a warm, practical, and sensitive way, cuddling her baby to her breast. When she does this she gives her baby exactly what he needs.

"She's a gorgeous baby— and so special. I could gaze at her for hours. It's hard to imagine being without her now. She's changed my life completely."

The mother and baby look into each other's eyes, engrossed in each other. The baby learns from her mother what it is to love and be loved. This first partnership is the basis of all trust and hope in life.

TRYING TO FOCUS

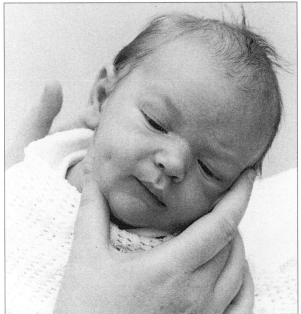

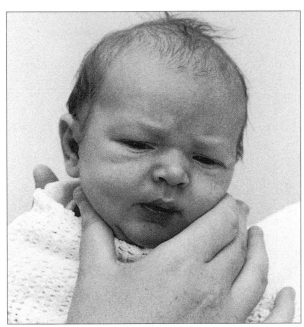

1 *When you hold your baby and look into his face, he may at first appear uninterested in you and look away. Don't hurry things. Wait patiently.*

2 *He will scan his field of vision, actively looking for something interesting. At first both eyes cannot coordinate easily. He looks baffled, but starts to search.*

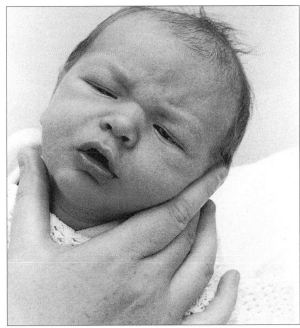

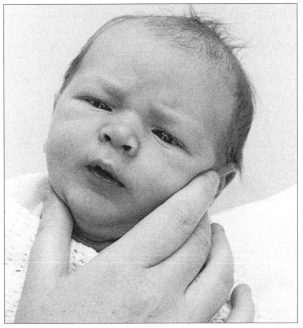

3 *Then he catches sight of you and squints as he tries to focus, for what he can see is fuzzy and blurred at the edges.*

4 *After some trial and error, he gazes at you with concentration and a slight frown, as if to say, "Is this really my mother?"*

The Sleepy Baby

After the hard work of birth a baby may sleep, waking only three or four times in the first 24 hours. Some babies are drowsy for days because of opiate drugs they have received during labor. A baby who is too hot may also be hard to rouse. Premature babies often need to be encouraged to latch on and suck, because they are sleepy, too. Occasionally a very sleepy baby who has reduced muscle tone is underfed and has become dehydrated, and this is obviously cause to worry.

HYPOGLYCEMIA (LOW BLOOD SUGAR)

A baby may also be sleepy because his blood sugar is low. Definitions of this condition are vague, and some babies are treated as having low blood sugar when they are perfectly normal, often because of inaccurate testing. A healthy, full-term baby does not need to be tested for low blood sugar.

Women are given conflicting advice, and babies are often fed formula milk in an effort to treat hypoglycemia. This does not work and it interferes with breastfeeding. Mothers of breastfed babies who were fed artificial milk in the hospital are three times more likely to give up breastfeeding in the first two weeks than those whose babies were not given formula.* If you are told that your baby has hypoglycemia, breastfeed more often.

STIMULATING THE BABY TO FEED

There are several things you can do to stimulate a sleepy baby to take the breast. It helps if she can bring her hands to her face to wake herself up, so make sure her hands are free.*

Talk to, stroke, and woo her. Partially undress her so that her feet are cool. This wakes some babies up immediately. Turn off bright lights and feed in half-light. Babies open their eyes and are more interested in their surroundings when the light is not glaring. Tease the baby with the breast by squeezing out a few drops of milk so that she can smell and lick it.

You could also explore what happens if you are both in a warm bath. Place her lying on your tummy, dribble warm water over her, play with her. She may creep up toward your breast.

You will know when she is ready for a feed because her eyes move quickly—even if they are still closed—she makes little movements with her mouth, tongue, and other parts of her body, brings her hands toward each other, makes chirping noises, and roots for the breast, turning her head from side to side and twisting her mouth. As soon as she is alert, offer your breast. Don't wait until she is crying, or she may get confused and distressed, fail to latch on, and cry until she is exhausted.

If your milk ejection reflex is slow to come and the baby loses interest before you feel a tingly, buzzing sensation, apply a warm towel or diaper to your breast before feeding.

Occasionally, a baby who has already become accustomed to a bottle manages more easily at the breast if you use a latex nipple shield. Once the baby is sucking well, and has paused for a moment, you slip the nipple shield off and latch her on to your breast.

Feeding problems are usually at the bottom of an apparent mismatch between a mother and her baby. Mothering is very difficult when a baby is not eager and responsive, and seems to reject your breast. It is easy to lose confidence and feel that the baby does not like you.

When a baby is able to draw in a good mouthful of breast so that milk flows copiously, her character often changes. A passive, sleepy baby becomes wide-awake and interested in her surroundings. After a few satisfying feeds, her muscle tone improves, you see a bloom and freshness on her skin, her eyes shine, and she takes each feed with gusto. Your relationship with the baby blossoms, as does your confidence.

A baby who is often only half awake (opposite), *and not at all sure that he wants to feed may need some encouragement.*

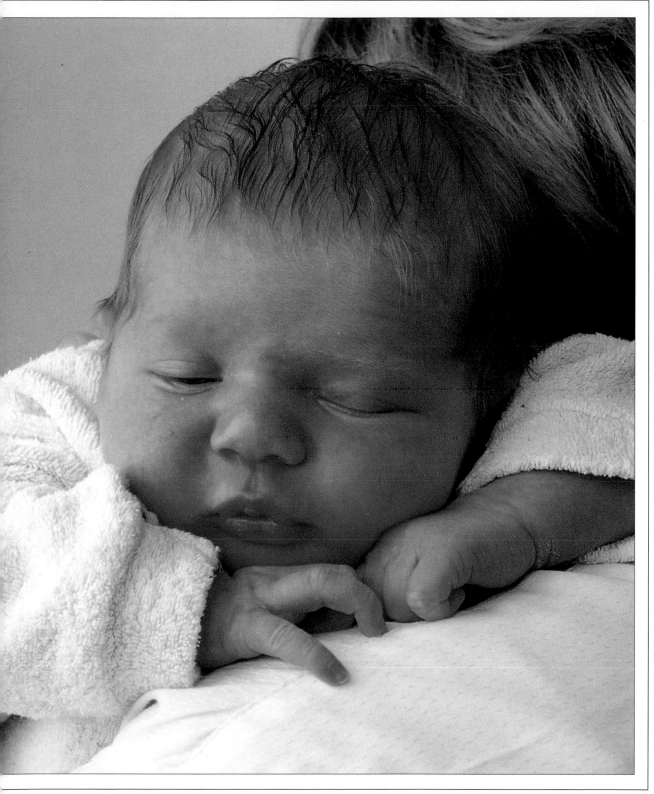

How to Encourage a Baby to Feed

Find a comfortable position. If it is easiest to sit, sit up with a straight back and pillows to support you. You can cradle your breast from underneath with the hand on the same side resting against your ribcage. If a breast is very full, express a little milk from it so that the area around your nipple becomes softer.

If your baby is small or your breasts are small, place a pillow on your lap so that the baby is at a level where his nose, rather than his mouth, is in line with your nipple.

Talk to your baby. See if you can make eye contact. Stroke his head, and trace the lines of his nose, eyebrows, ears, and mouth with your fingers, talking to him all the time and noticing how he responds.

When fully awake he may start rooting for the breast. Choose the moment when his mouth is wide open and use the hand opposite the breast from which you are going to feed to support the baby's head and guide him onto the breast. His chin should be raised, and the lower jaw should make contact with the breast first (see pages 30–39).

Once your baby is obtaining milk there is a special rhythm: a short burst of sucking, a pause, then a few deep, long sucks, followed by another pause, some quick sucks, a round of deep sucks again, and so on. During the pauses, avoid distracting or jiggling the baby. These pauses are a natural part of the pattern of breastfeeding. Bottle-fed babies tend to suck steadily, but pauses are a vital element in the breastfeeding rhythm. As the feed continues, these pauses often become longer.

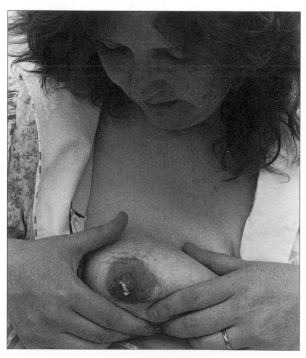

ENTICING YOUR BABY TO FEED

1 *Talk to your baby. Show him things that shine or move. See if you can make eye contact. Stroke his head, and trace the lines of his nose, eyebrows, ears, and mouth with your fingers, talking to him all the time.*

2 *Squeeze out a little milk so it glistens like a pearl on the surface of your nipple. Tantalize your baby with it. When he smells how delicious it is, he may become interested enough to suck.*

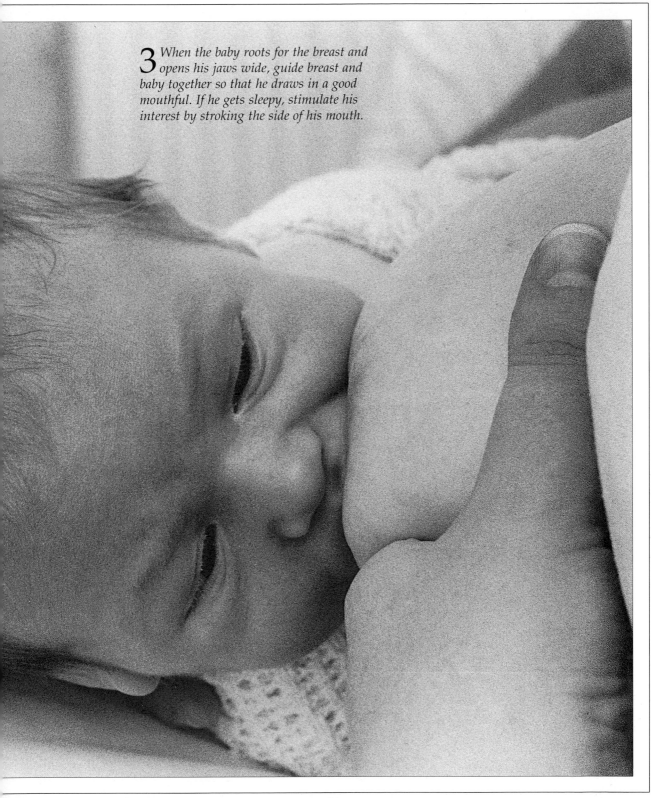

3 When the baby roots for the breast and opens his jaws wide, guide breast and baby together so that he draws in a good mouthful. If he gets sleepy, stimulate his interest by stroking the side of his mouth.

The Excited Baby

An excited baby may need to be calmed down before she will take the breast. If your baby cries furiously for food, but then resists being put to the breast, arching her back, pummeling you with her fists, and turning purple with rage, don't struggle with her. Do something quite different, such as changing the diaper or putting her over your shoulder and patting her bottom, until she has quieted down. Or hand her to someone else for a few minutes; it may be that she is stimulated by your own body scent, the smell of your milk, and the nearness of your breasts.

THE REJECTED BREAST

Sometimes a baby comes to the breast, starts to suck, and then pulls away as if you were feeding her poison. Your milk ejection reflex may be delayed. She can't wait to get at the milk. Don't panic! That will make things worse.

Gently massage your breast and warm it with a hot facecloth or an electric heating pad. This can be quite an acrobatic task with a distressed baby in your arms, so either lay the baby across your lap or ask someone else to hold her while you do this. If another person is holding the baby, she should be in a position different from that used when she is put to the breast, so that she is not confused.

Express a little milk. It will increase your confidence to see it. Now offer the breast again. Make sure that the baby's body is in a straight line and that she does not have to twist to get at the breast. You should be tummy to tummy and chest to chest, and the baby's mouth should be gaping wide as you place her on the breast so that her lower jaw is well under your areola. Now she can get at the milk, and it is flowing fast!

SOOTHING A FRETFUL BABY

A baby who is restless and fretful but not actually screaming often quiets down if you rest your head against hers and hum a resonant tune or just a few deep, melodious sounds. As soon as she is contented, offer the breast gently but quickly.

Some babies get overstimulated and react with distress to every unexpected sound and movement, as well as to hunger and digestive processes inside them. They may cry and fight the breast, and need to be calmed before being nursed.

WRAPPING AN EXCITED BABY

1 *An overexcited newborn baby may calm down eventually if wrapped in a large, soft shawl, towel, or receiving blanket. Here, an experienced midwife places the baby on a big shawl on her lap and begins to wrap him up. She talks soothingly as she does so, telling him what a beautiful baby he is.*

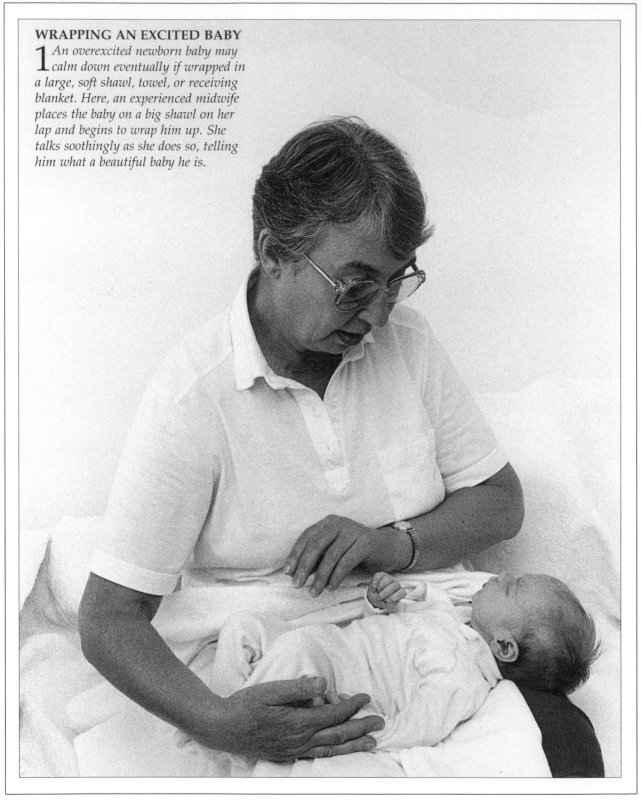

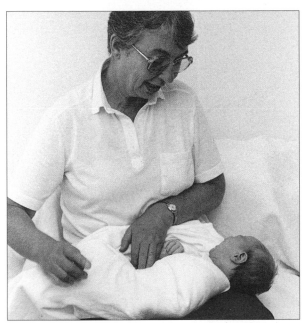

2 *She draws up one side of the shawl and tucks it tightly around the baby, moving slowly and deliberately and talking softly all the time.*

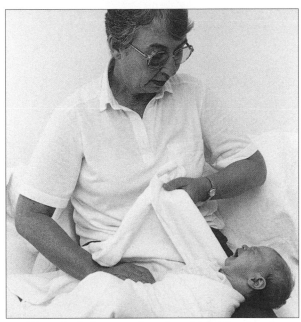

3 *Then she brings up the other side of the shawl, quietly and confidently, and tucks the baby's arms firmly against his body.*

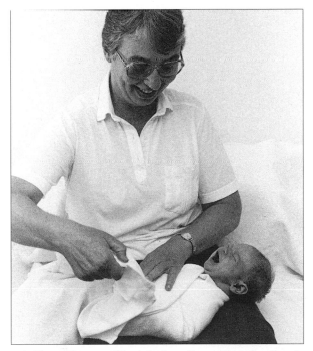

4 *She makes a solid, tight bundle, so that the shawl holds the baby rather as the muscles of the uterus must have grasped him before birth.*

Babies who are very easily stimulated often like to feed in a room with only dim light, or with their eyes protected by a shawl, and they sometimes like a background of soothing music. If your baby is like this, see if you can go to a quiet room away from other people so that your baby can feed peacefully.

Some babies get so angry in their first weeks, and seem so frightened by their anger, that they are happiest when cocooned firmly in a big towel or blanket with only the head visible (see left and above).

Babies undergo all sorts of uncomfortable experiences, many of which are unavoidable since they are connected with internal sensations and with the baby's adjustment to life. A baby who is bombarded by stimuli from inside cannot really concentrate on the outside world and on the things you are doing to help her. But one of the most important things you can do for your baby—from birth onward—is to reach out to comfort her as soon as she becomes distressed. You won't always manage to soothe her. But at least she knows you are trying.

Digestive Adventures

Babies are often overwhelmed by their digestive processes and all the alarming things that are going on inside them.

ADAPTING TO THE OUTSIDE WORLD

Before birth the baby is fed automatically from your bloodstream as nutritious elements percolate through the placenta directly into his bloodstream. Not only does he not have to do any work to get fed, but the food is instantly available, without even a half-second pause. In fact, it flows continuously into his body. So it must feel odd to your newborn baby to have things squeezing and bumping, opening and constricting inside him when he is not used to it.

As milk goes down the esophagus, it is helped toward the stomach by regular muscular tightening of the tube. The milk residue enters the intestines and is directed down to the lower bowel in the same way. These actions often become unsynchronized, especially if the baby has been gulping hungrily or crying furiously. Sometimes it seems to happen if the mother has eaten foods to which the baby is not yet accustomed. All these new digestive adventures your baby is experiencing are clearly visible to you—he may screw up his face in surprise, frown, squirm, writhe, and become miserable.

COMFORTING YOUR BABY

A baby who is engrossed in a digestive experience like this is best held upright against your shoulder or laid down on his tummy on your lap. Pat him on the bottom with a slow, regular rhythm. Warmth may help—rest a covered hot water bottle a little warmer than body temperature, or a facecloth wrung out in hot water, against his tummy. But make sure that nothing is too hot, as babies scald easily.

Talk soothing nonsense words to him, or sing softly, so that the baby hears from the tone of your voice and learns from your own confidence that these internal events are not catastrophic and will soon pass.

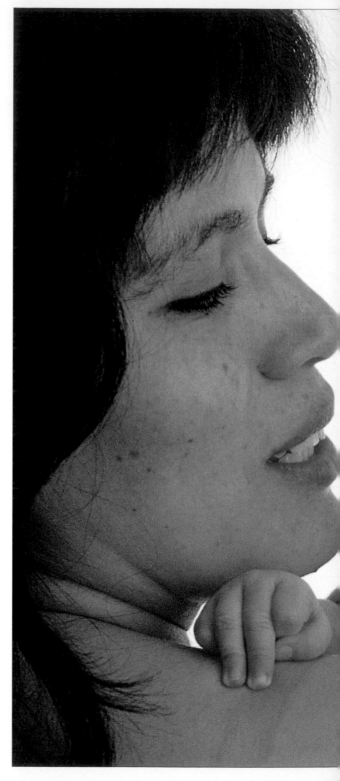

A baby may feel bombarded by strange
and unsettling sensations going on inside her
during the process of digestion. She may feel
uncomfortable and even frightened. Holding
the baby upright over your shoulder or on
your lap helps her feel safe; soon she will
come to accept the extraordinary feelings.

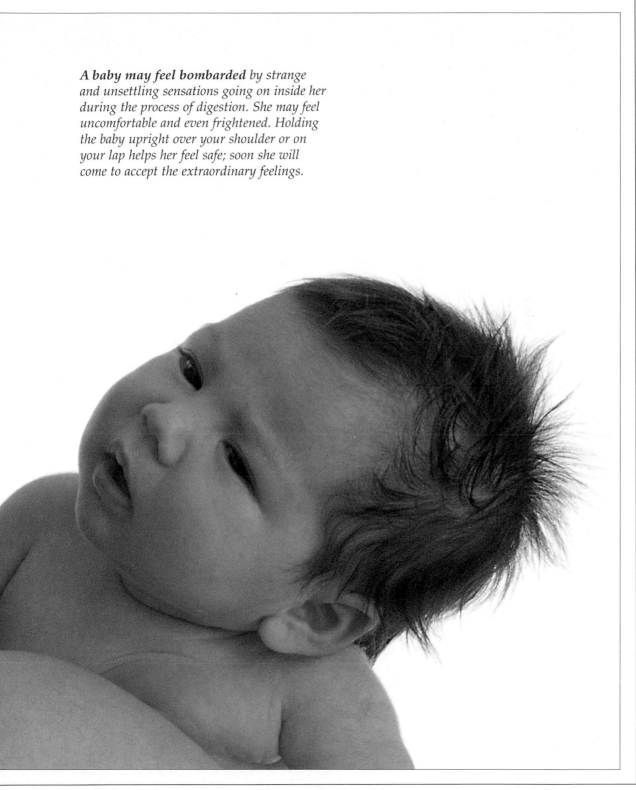

When It's Hard to Love a Baby

Some babies are difficult to love. They seem to ignore you, or they cry inconsolably, or they are like aliens from another planet. You may feel that you lack all maternal instincts, blame yourself, and feel guilty about this.

Falling in love with a baby can take time. As with any love affair, you may fall head over heels in love from the moment you first hold a baby in your arms, or love may unfold more slowly over weeks and months. You cannot hurry it. You need time with your baby when you can cuddle close, stroke her, look into her eyes, and learn about her.

AFTER A TRAUMATIC BIRTH

When a woman has had a traumatic birth, she may go through a transitional period, often lasting some months, but sometimes longer, when she suffers from post-traumatic stress disorder (PTSD). She relives the birth in her thoughts, has panic attacks, flashbacks, and violent mood swings and is very frightened. She feels very alone and cannot share her thoughts with other mothers who all seem to be coping better. She may not be able to help thinking that her baby is responsible for this.

If you have been disempowered in childbirth, it can leave you feeling helpless as a mother, too. You weren't in control then, and you feel you've lost control now. You feel that you have no right to be a mother. The baby may seem a tyrant who has you in her power.

Go to your doctor, and ask if there is a counselor attached to the practice who you can talk to. Or your doctor may refer you to a psychiatrist who understands these problems.

DEPRESSION AND ANGER

Depression also affects a woman's relationship with a baby. She often switches off emotionally. Depression is different from PTSD, but if a woman does not have help with PTSD it often turns into depression. A depressed woman feels there is an invisible barrier, like a glass wall, between her and the baby. If you are going through an emotionally testing time, if you worry that you are an inadequate mother and take no joy in your baby, reach out and ask for help. Meanwhile, act the part of a good mother, and you will become one. Although you may feel like a robot, continue to cuddle, touch, talk to, and sing to your baby and it will gradually become rewarding.

Sometimes a woman feels uncontrollable anger against a baby, especially a baby who cries, and who does not respond to her attempts to calm her. If this is the case with you, put the baby down in a safe place and leave the room. Play music as a sound barrier or turn on the TV. Use slow, regular, full breathing, with the emphasis on the breath out, until you are peaceful again. Tell your doctor that you need help, confide in someone close, and see if you can get help with child care.

ANXIETY

A woman may be so anxious about her baby, and afraid that she may harm her, that she distances herself from her. She freezes her baby out because she is terrified of her own power over this new life. If you feel like this, you need someone with you all the time who takes main responsibility for care of the baby, while you participate in all decisions and tackle one simple task at a time, at your own pace.

Women often worry that if they let anyone know that they are finding mothering difficult, the baby will be taken from them. It is true that if a woman is hostile toward or neglects her baby, separation may be advised while she has medical treatment. But increasingly, psychiatrists and social workers try to keep a mother and baby together. Seek help soon, rather than leaving it until you feel desperate.

Having a baby is a major life transition. It is not surprising that it proves stressful. For many women, it is a time when they confront emotional problems stemming from how they think about themselves, their relationships, and their baby. But with loving care and, if necessary, with expert help, this distress usually fades within weeks.

"Oliver nestles against me and I hum a tune. I think he likes to feel the reverberation of my humming through the bones of his head."

Introducing Other Pleasures

You do not have to put the baby to the breast every time she cries. In the first two or three weeks of life, crying can probably be assuaged only by giving the breast, but after that the world opens up and new delights blossom. If all you ever offer your baby is the breast, you may not discover other ways of giving him pleasure.

NEW EXPERIENCES

When your baby is restless he may want something other than food—to be cuddled, for example, to float in warm water, to move to another position, or perhaps to kick on his back with no clothes on. Or he may like to have a soothing massage, listen to music or a tinkling bell, or watch a dancing mobile or shadows on the wall. Early on, your baby learns that there are other pleasures in life besides breastfeeding. If you can see when he is ready for a variety of new learning experiences, you will contribute to him becoming an integrated human being who is secure in himself and who can use his environment for more learning.

If you are very tired, you probably feel that feeding is just about all you can do, and that you haven't the time for anything else except laundry and basic housework. However, doing things with your baby, playing with him, watching him develop, receiving responses from him, and sometimes being rewarded with a smile or a chuckle—this makes the hard work and the broken nights worthwhile. So even if you are feeling overtired, it is important for you both that you have time to enjoy each other.

BATH TIME

Bathing your baby is one of those special activities that can be the high point of the day for you both. (In fact, there is no reason why a baby cannot have several baths a day.) Putting a baby in a warm, comforting bath is one of the best ways of breaking tension and helps him—and you—to relax. Until you are confident of your judgment, test the water with a thermometer; it should be as warm as your baby's body (around 85°F). Ensure that the room is comfortably warm, too. Heat up a big soft bath towel and bundle him up cosily in it after the bath. Never leave a baby in a bath unattended, however much he enjoys it, even though you are just on the other side of the door.

Some babies experience near ecstasy in the bath. They can move freely, kick vigorously, and make exciting splashes (and the occasional tidal wave), all with an adoring audience. They soon learn to close their eyes to keep out the water. A baby may enjoy lying unsupported in shallow water, but never leave him alone.

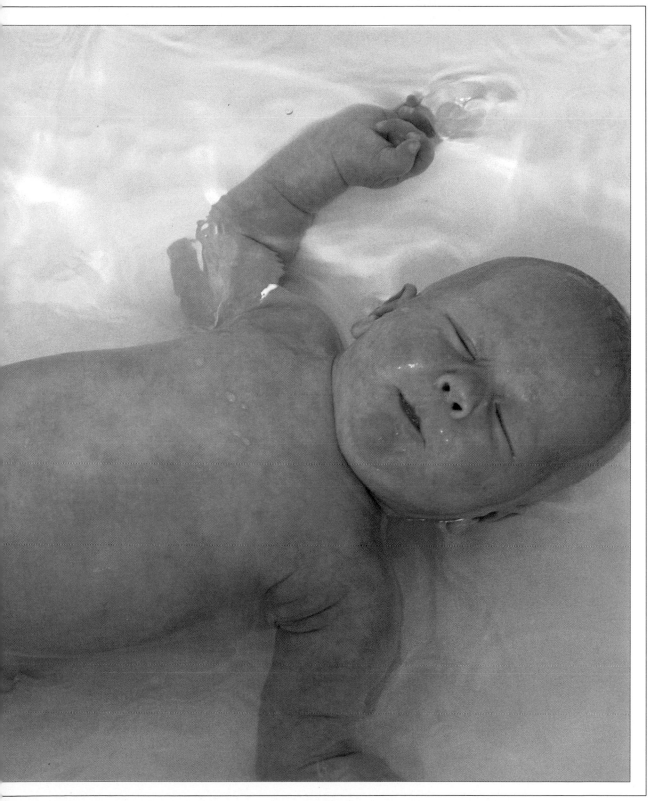

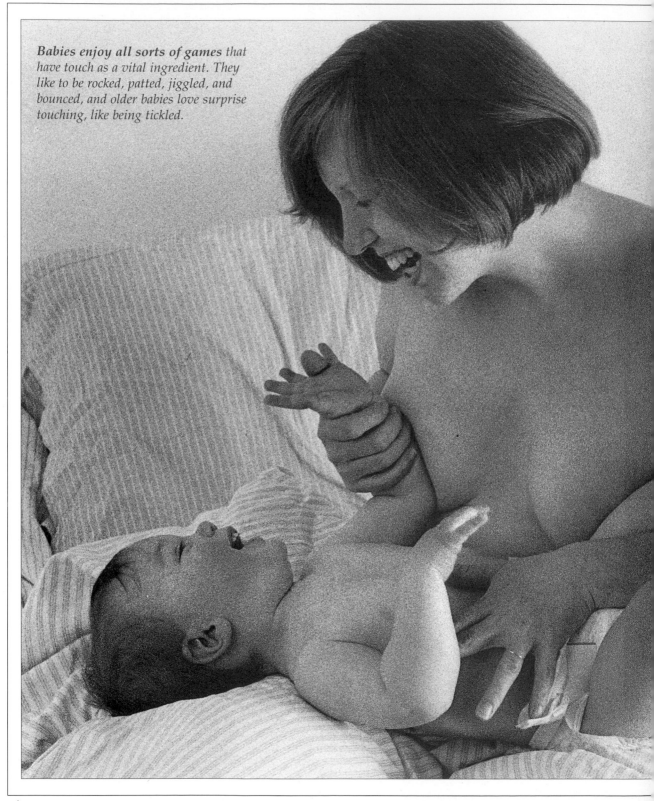

Babies enjoy all sorts of games that have touch as a vital ingredient. They like to be rocked, patted, jiggled, and bounced, and older babies love surprise touching, like being tickled.

It is important to offer new pleasures only when the baby is calm, happy, and responsive. Do not push things. Just wait and see what happens, and enjoy it when your baby's attention is focused, his eyes light up, and he eagerly reaches out to grasp new and exciting experiences.

STIMULATING THE SENSES

Even when a baby is only a few days old, he will enjoy having his senses stimulated in different ways while he's in a quiet, alert state. He may like to smell a lemon, or freshly ground coffee, or herbs, garlic, or lavender from the garden. Present each scent separately and simply give the baby the opportunity to concentrate on experiencing it.

Long before you introduce solid foods, your baby may like to smell, and even taste, a variety of things: a peeled cherry, perhaps, or a strawberry, or a grape. Do not put them in the baby's mouth. Rest the object lightly against his lips and observe what happens. Even a baby of a few weeks old may like a few licks of a frozen juice pop if the weather is hot. But be alert to possible allergic reactions (see page 150). Give the baby plenty of time to savor and appreciate the taste and smell of the new experience you are presenting.

LOOKING AND LEARNING

Babies have strong visual preferences. They do not stare passively at anything and everything. They select what interests them. They enjoy the play of light and shadow on a wall. They gaze with concentrated pleasure at textured fabrics and intricate patterns. They prefer patterned to plain surfaces, even if the plain ones are brightly colored, and they like three-dimensional objects and things that move. Show your baby swirls and zigzags, stripes, squares, circles, and diamonds—anything with a strong pattern. Patchwork is a never-failing source of delight. Babies also like to see lace and muslin move in the breeze, which is why cradles hung with lace and frilly things were not just pretty domestic ornaments, but met babies' needs for visual stimulation.

Your baby is also busy learning about you and everyone else around him. He watches people's eyes and mouths and hears the sounds they produce. He copies the shapes formed by their mouths, smiles, and receives a smile in return. He learns to anticipate other people's behavior—knowing that when bathwater is running, something good is about to happen, that when he is put on his back in a certain way he is about to have a diaper changed, or that when settled on his back he is expected to go to sleep.

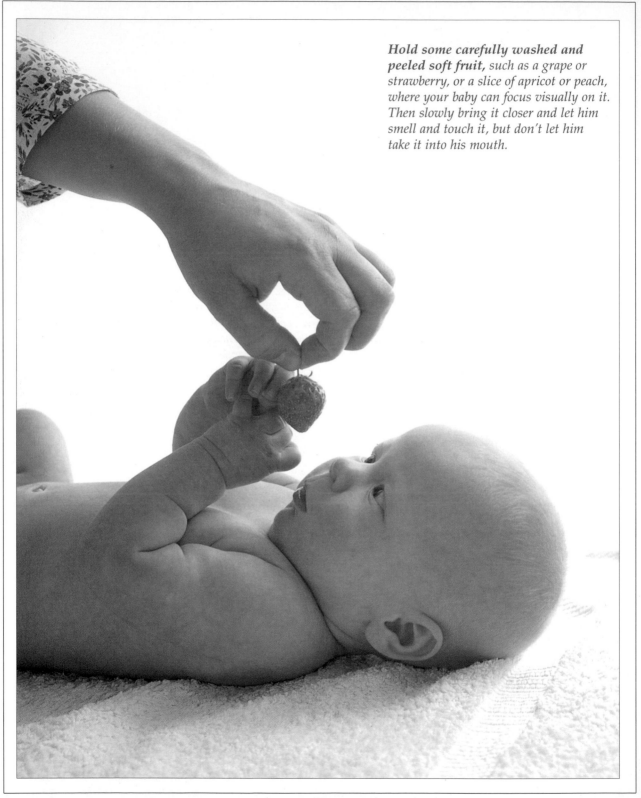

Hold some carefully washed and peeled soft fruit, such as a grape or strawberry, or a slice of apricot or peach, where your baby can focus visually on it. Then slowly bring it closer and let him smell and touch it, but don't let him take it into his mouth.

Sounds

A baby is born with hearing already attuned to particular sounds. Your own voice, your partner's voice, the voices of your other children, are all fascinating, especially if words, phrases, and cadences are repeated. If you have been watching a TV soap opera or a radio program regularly that is introduced by a particular jingle, or if you have played music to your baby while in utero, he or she will often grow quiet and look intrigued when you play this music again. Parents have described how their baby has concentrated on the sound of a guitar or drum that they played regularly during pregnancy.

Babies like repetition, reverberation, and a strong rhythm. They can find the hum of machinery comforting, provided it is not too loud, as well as the repeated flushing of the toilet and the sound of running water.

Your baby will enjoy being held above you and having a different view. While you talk or sing to him, he will find it exciting to be held (above) and then suddenly to be swept down so that you can kiss him or rub noses (below).

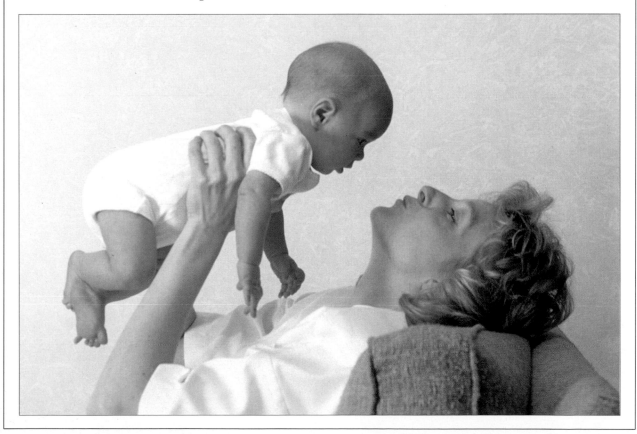

Talking to your baby *will encourage him to respond and talk to you, and in this way he will begin to learn language. He also imitates your facial expressions and mouth shapes, just as you copy his.*

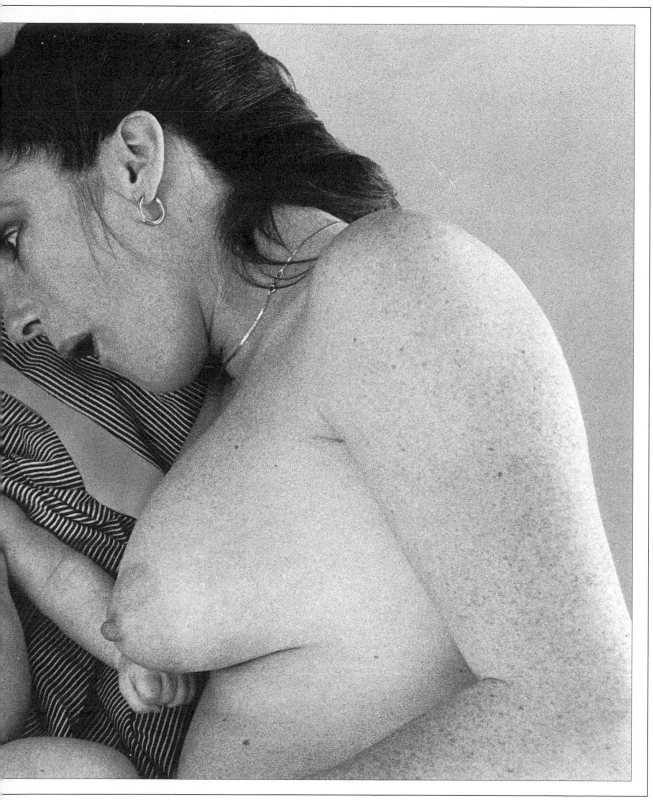

THE BABY WITH SPECIAL NEEDS

The Baby in the Special-Care Nursery

PREMATURE BABIES MAY NOT LOOK at all cuddly. Even full-term babies who are ill or are born with a disability may look so pathetic that you feel sorry for them, rather than feeling a rush of love. This can easily affect your feelings about breastfeeding. You may feel guilty that you have harmed your baby by giving birth too soon, or because he is not physically perfect. You may feel repelled by the baby's appearance and by all the equipment surrounding him.

The baby may be in an incubator, wrapped in foil or plastic, or may be lying naked under a heater, with a bright-red body and sprawling limbs. It may be difficult to see his face because he has a hat pulled down low to prevent heat loss. Tubes and wires may be sticking out everywhere.

Ask the nurses to explain what the wires, tubes, knobs, dials, and lights are for. Ask the pediatrician about the baby's treatment. Repeat questions if the answers are vague and don't give you enough information, or if you do not understand them. Asking questions will help you keep in touch with what is happening.

BENEFITS OF BREASTMILK

Your premature or ill baby will benefit from being given your own breastmilk, even if he is being fed by tube. When a baby is premature, the milk you produce has a higher protein content than if he was full-term, so your milk is especially suited to his needs. Breastmilk protects against necrotizing enterocolitis (the condition in which a baby has severe diarrhea with blood appearing in the stools). It is six times as common in formula-fed as in breastfed babies.*

Let the nurse in charge know that you want to breastfeed and, if the baby cannot suck, that you wish to express breastmilk for tube feeds.

Ask the midwife or nurse in the postnatal ward for help with learning how to express your colostrum and, later, milk. Start expressing as soon as you like after the birth; if there is no breast pump immediately available, massage and express milk by hand (see page 136).

To build up a good supply you will need to express milk for five to eight minutes from each breast, five or six times a day. This milk can be dripped into a tube that has been inserted through the baby's nose and down into his stomach. The tube is fixed with sticky tape to his cheek and is kept there between feeds.

THE BREASTMILK BANK

At first, until your milk supply is established, your breastmilk may be mixed with expressed breastmilk—donated by other mothers— from the hospital milk bank. It is heated to 144.5°F for 30 minutes to destroy any harmful bacteria or viruses that may be present, including the AIDS virus. Then it is frozen at -0.4°F or lower. Deep-freezing reduces some of the anti-infective properties of breastmilk, but does not otherwise change it.

If the hospital does not have a milk bank, you may be able to arrange to get expressed milk from mothers in your area through the Human Milk Banking Association (see page 164).

You may soon find that you are expressing more milk than your baby can take. The extra milk should be put in a small plastic container, labeled with your name and the baby's, and frozen for future use.

FEEDING A PREMATURE BABY

Sometimes a baby is well enough to be taken out of the plastic box or crib for short intervals from the beginning, so you can cuddle and talk to him and even feed him. Do not feel under pressure to get the baby fixed to the breast at first. Enjoy your baby and start to get to know each other. When your baby is ready to suck, it will probably only be for a very short time at

In many special-care baby units, mothers can help to feed their premature babies before they leave the hospital. Here a new mother feeds one of her premature twins expressed breastmilk through a fine nasogastric tube taped to the baby's cheek. She controls the flow of milk with the fingers of her right hand.

first, as he will tire quickly. Put him to the breast, and when he starts finding it hard work, finish, if necessary, by tube feeding with expressed milk. Though it is exciting to know that the baby is sucking at last, it is a very slow process, and you may feel depressed and very tired yourself.

A premature or ill baby may have to be taught how to latch on to the breast correctly and even how to suck (see pages 30–39). To help stimulate the correct movement of the jaw when your baby is getting tired, put a finger under his chin and exert gentle pressure.

Your baby will be test-weighed at each feed to see how much he is drinking and to determine whether your milk needs supplementing. Some pediatricians recommend supplements for all premature babies, no matter how much milk their mothers produce: you may want to discuss this.

You will need to find out exactly what your baby's feeding schedule is, so that you can be in the nursery at the right times to put him to the breast. It can be very upsetting to arrive there only to find that the baby has been fed and is now asleep and that you are dismissed.

Even when your baby is sucking well at the breast, continue to use the pump at the end of each feed, as this will stimulate your milk supply. Go on doing this until breastfeeding is well established and you feel confident.

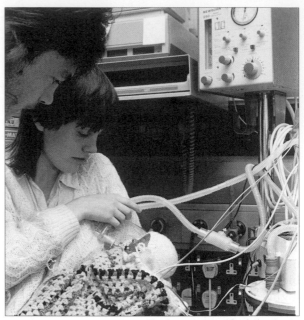

Feeding your premature baby yourself while she is in the high-tech setting of a special-care unit helps you feel that she belongs to you.

GOING HOME

The time comes for you to take your baby home. If you first spend a few days in the hospital living with your baby and feeding whenever he wants the breast, you will get to know him better as a person, and your relationship will be established. Some hospitals have beds for mothers in or beside the special-care baby unit, where they can get help with feeding and caring for their premature babies.

Ask the hospital to freeze any expressed milk that remains, as it may be useful at home. If your baby gets tired at the breast, you can finish with a bottle of your own milk. Bottle-feeding can ask less effort from the baby than breastfeeding, and it may take a few weeks before your baby can satisfy his appetite fully at the breast.

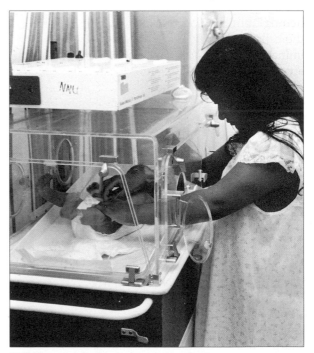

While your baby is in an incubator, you can change her diaper and gently stroke and massage her through the portholes.

The Jaundiced Baby

If your three- or four-day-old baby looks as if he has just come back from a holiday in the tropics and is beautifully tanned, the chances are that he has jaundice. Four or five babies in every ten develop some yellowing of the eyes and of the skin—especially on the legs—at this time, which gradually fades until it disappears entirely when they are a week or two old (see page 158).

CAUSES OF JAUNDICE

Most of these babies are completely healthy. This "physiological" jaundice occurs because of the breakdown of red cells in the baby's blood. While in the uterus, your baby has a higher proportion of red blood cells than he needs after birth. This enables him to get good oxygenation inside your body.

During pregnancy the placenta filters out waste products from the red blood cells. Once the baby is born his own liver must break down hemoglobin, the oxygen-carrying molecule in the cells, so that it can be expelled. Until the immature liver can do this fast enough, bilirubin, a yellow pigment that is a byproduct of this process, builds up in the tissues. When the bilirubin level gets very high, brain damage can result, so jaundiced babies are watched carefully.

The chances of a baby's developing jaundice are increased when the mother has taken certain drugs (including aspirin, tranquilizers, diuretics, antibiotics, steroids, and sulfa drugs), when labor has been induced or accelerated with an oxytocin intravenous drip, or if she had epidural anesthesia.

TREATMENT OF JAUNDICE

The treatment for jaundice is abundant fluids, which means breastfeeding frequently. Bilirubin is light-sensitive and light therapy can be used. It entails putting the baby under bright artificial light to reduce the serum bilirubin in the blood and tissues. Usually, the baby, who has been blindfolded so that the eyes cannot be damaged, is placed under an ordinary fluorescent light. If you are at home, you can achieve the same effect by laying your baby naked in warm sunlight in the backyard or on a balcony. Research on the value of light treatment was started after a nurse noticed that babies put by a window, where sunlight streamed in on them, had less jaundice than those who were in cribs away from the light.

It has been observed that delayed passage of meconium, the first contents of the baby's bowels, is associated with higher levels of bilirubin. Meconium is passed sooner when a baby is breastfed frequently from birth. So the best way of preventing jaundice is to start feeding shortly after birth and to feed often without any supplementation.*

It used to be assumed that jaundiced babies should be given water, but research has demonstrated that there is no benefit in this for breastfed babies.* Though supplementary water does not prevent jaundice, mothers are often told that they should persuade their babies to drink water "just in case." But giving anything at all in addition to your own milk interferes with the smooth start of breastfeeding, and may reduce milk production and get the baby hooked on the bottle. A jaundiced baby is usually sleepy and may need to be woken for breastfeeds every two hours during the day.

BREASTMILK JAUNDICE

There is a rare kind of jaundice known as "breastmilk jaundice," where a mother's milk causes a rise in bilirubin in her baby's tissues. This condition is overdiagnosed, but if the pediatrician thinks that your baby has this, there is still no need to give up breastfeeding. You will need to interrupt breastfeeding for, at most, 24 hours, to enable the bilirubin level to go down; you may be asked to repeat this in successive weeks. While the baby is being bottle-fed, express your milk regularly in order to keep up your milk supply. Perhaps the baby can be fed expressed breastmilk from a milk bank or can be breastfed by another mother while you are unable to feed.

Babies with Disabilities

For any baby who finds it difficult to develop the neuromuscular coordination needed for sucking and swallowing, learning to breastfeed is a challenge, and it can be tiring for you both.

The mother has to establish a good milk supply with a lively milk ejection reflex. That means expressing milk regularly to make up for the baby's feeble sucking, either after each breastfeed or in place of breastfeeds, while the baby is tube-fed or fed by bottle or spoon. It is possible to lactate for months on end using expression alone, though you have to be very committed to it. The baby cannot shape a bottle teat in the same way as flexible breast tissue. If a baby has difficulty in coordinating tongue, jaw, and swallowing and breathing movements, it may be easier to breastfeed, because she can mold the breast into the most convenient shape.

DOWN'S SYNDROME AND CEREBRAL PALSY

For a baby with Down's syndrome or cerebral palsy, breastfeeding may be best if you can get over the initial difficulties.

Some Down's syndrome babies breastfeed well from the start. Others take awhile to become coordinated. Some never manage it at all. These may be babies who also have heart conditions, a problem that affects 50 percent of Down's babies.

Express your milk at first (see page 136). You will have time to help the baby breastfeed.

CLEFT PALATE

A baby with a cleft palate often cannot easily form the breast into a nipple shape because she cannot create a vacuum between breast and mouth. If the cleft is not central, or if it is short, she can block the cleft with the breast. You may need to start breastfeeding wearing a flexible nipple shield, which has the effect of artificially enlarging the areola and nipple. Sometimes the baby is fitted with a small plastic plate to correct the shape of the hard palate. But babies usually need the sensation of the breast against the palate and become distressed without it.

If you maintain your milk supply until after the baby has had an operation to repair the palate, you may be able to start breastfeeding afterward. Immediately following the operation you can give your baby expressed milk using a bottle with a spoon attachment. Milk flows from the bottle into the spoon, from where you can control the flow of milk into your baby's mouth.

There are many different kinds of synthetic nipples on the market (see example below). The American Cleft Palate Association can give you information about these as well as advice about feeding (see page 164).

You may be anxious if milk goes up her nose before she swallows. This does not matter. If she coughs or chokes, feed more slowly.

CARDIAC DEFECT

A baby with a heart defect and metabolic illness may be able to breastfeed. One who is receiving oxygen therapy can breastfeed with a nasal tube still in place. But the neonatologist and cardiologist may advise you to bottle-feed, believing that breastfeeding is more stressful for the baby. Research shows, however, that in general, for premature babies breastfeeding does not use more energy, as long as the milk is flowing well.

VALVE SYSTEM FEEDER

Slit valve controls the flow of milk.

Markings show the position of the slit valve in your baby's mouth and indicate the flow rate.

Reservoir fills with milk; use light finger pressure to squeeze milk into your baby's mouth.

Standard bottle

Babies who have difficulty feeding because of problems such as cleft palate, a heart condition, or neurological weakness, can be helped with this nipple that attaches to an ordinary bottle.

Disc valve inside the collar means there is only a forward flow, which helps babies who suck weakly.

"Sophie is seven months old. Every day I give her a full massage using oil for 20 minutes or more. This daily sense of her body has helped her with motor development. She is a difficult feeder, constantly pulling off, shouting, and looking around the room. So I have to feed her little and often."

THE MOTHER & BABY RELATIONSHIP

The Baby's Emotional Experience

MOST OF A BABY'S LIFE HAS TO DO WITH feeding and all the things connected with feeding. There is hunger and the longing for food, the excitement of taking the breast into the mouth, pleasure as milk squirts against the soft palate, the satisfaction of sucking and swallowing, and the delicious feeling as the milk goes down and the baby's tummy becomes full. Then there are all the processes involved in digestion: sensations of pressure, bubbles of gas, rhythms of the tightening of the gut, and the surprising events that occur at the other end, producing warm liquid and solid matter as if by magic.

THE PLEASURE OF FEEDING
When you watch a baby at the breast who is enjoying a feed, it is clear that all his attention, every muscle and nerve fiber, every atom of his being, is focused on a thrilling and sensuous activity. Dr. Donald Winnicott, a pediatrician and psychiatrist, once remarked that when

breastfeeding is going well, "The whole of the emerging personality is engaged."* Feeding can be done mechanically by a mother who nurses in a detached, unresponsive way. However, if a mother is not paying her baby any attention and is thinking of other things, then it may be so boring for the baby that it is a relief for him to cry with anger and frustration. Babies have very effective ways of demanding our attention.

COMMUNICATION OF FEELINGS
Bottle-feeding can be a fulfilling experience for a baby, too, when it is done with sensitivity and closeness. An important element is the mother's attention and the way she concentrates on her baby, at least intermittently, as they look into each other's eyes. An additional part of the overall experience of breastfeeding, however, is the taste, smell, and feel of the breast from which the delicious milk flows freely.

Everything a mother is feeling as the baby sucks at her breast is part of the baby's experience, too. These feelings are communicated spontaneously through her eyes and mouth, in the way that she holds her baby, by the movements of her body, and in her voice and her breathing. From all that a mother gives her baby in these ways, the baby begins to learn about life and to have rich and varied emotional experiences. The early feeding relationship is so intense that it is the foundation of all other relationships later in life.

When a baby is at the breast (opposite), *he is unaware of anything that is going on around him, as, with eyes tightly closed, he is enveloped by a sensuous activity that is totally satisfying—the bliss of sucking.*

A baby enjoys being showered with kisses and *having a big bear hug (left). Knowing that she is loved is an important part of a baby's emotional experience and makes her feel secure and happy.*

Managing Your Time

When you first have a baby you may feel that you will never have time in your waking hours to do everything you need to do. A new baby can be a full-time job and more, since there is no point at which you can sign off. You are on duty 24 hours a day, and the difference between day and night becomes blurred. You may feel you have to rush feeds or put off the baby with a skimpy feed because you must do something else, but you will soon discover that the baby always seems to be aware of this and gets cross and restless. It is impossible to force schedules on a young baby. And even though you can discover the baby's rhythms, this is very difficult in the first three months. Babies often sleep and wake at unexpected times and need your immediate attention as their mouths open and, with eyes still tightly closed, they grope for the breast, knowing only that they want to be fed, and quickly.

FEELING GUILTY

Some women feel almost guilty about sitting down and feeding a baby because they ought to be cooking a meal, washing the dishes, hanging out the laundry, making the beds, tidying the living room, or vacuuming the floor. It is as if what they are doing is self-indulgent, or of secondary importance to housework. Other people, including an otherwise loving partner, may expect life to go on more or less as before the baby came, since in all cultures it is usually assumed that women have a natural ability for housework and can cope in all situations.

GETTING EXTRA HELP

However much help you had before, you need more now. When you are breastfeeding you are not resting, even if you are lying down or are curled up on a sofa. If you have never had much help from your partner there will have to be a massive change in the way you divide up the work between you. He will have to take over jobs he is not accustomed to doing, including things that he may protest he has never learned

to do, does not like doing, or does not do well at all. Now is the time to learn—fatherhood, like motherhood, is a great educator!

THE 24-HOUR PEAK PRODUCTION PLAN

Sometimes you need extra help because your baby is having a growth spurt and wants more milk, and you have to concentrate on feeding. You need some time to build up your milk supply, which you can accomplish in 24 hours. If you are back at work, see if you can get a day off. Maybe your partner can arrange time off, too. If that is impossible, use a weekend in which it is understood that breastfeeding is your top priority. If you do not have a partner, perhaps you can ask a family member or close friend to give you 24 hours so that you can go to bed and focus on your baby. If you have other children, arrange child care and special treats for at least some of the time, and put your and your baby's needs first. You will be more relaxed with your older children if you do not feel that you have to struggle on, regardless.

Take your baby into bed with you, let her wear only a diaper, and go topless yourself, so that you are in skin-to-skin contact. Whenever the baby seems interested in having a breastfeed, put her to the breast. Don't wait for her to cry. Either lie on your side or sit up straight. Avoid leaning back against pillows, since it is difficult to position a baby well when you are reclining. Encourage her to feed as long as she likes on one breast and then put her to the other. Then go back to the first breast again, which by this time will have started producing milk again. She may want to feed every two to three hours. In 24 hours you will have built up your milk supply.

If your baby is drowsy with a cold or ear infection and cannot suck for long, express milk when she has dropped off the breast. Keep this milk in the fridge. It will be rich in cream and provide extra calories for your baby. Feed it by bottle or with a cup and spoon, or, if your baby is already eating solid food, mix it with cereal.

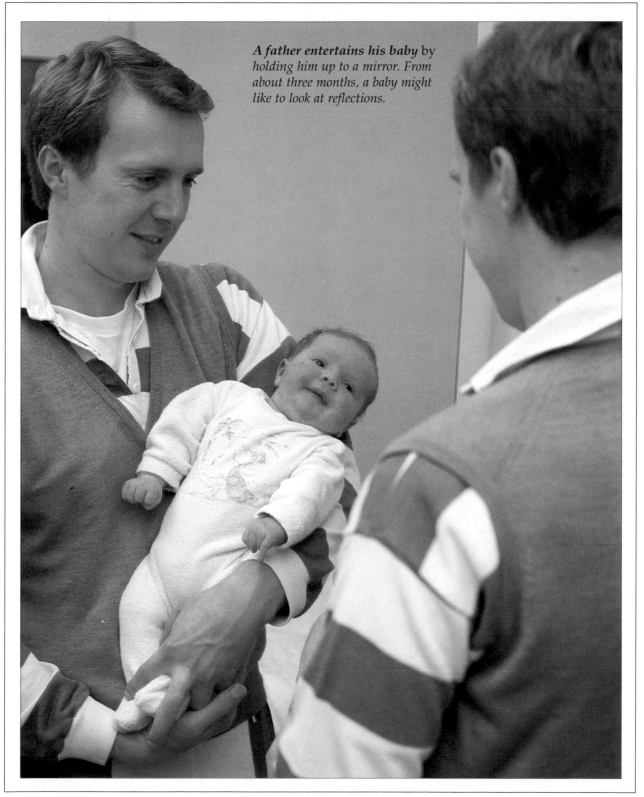

A father entertains his baby by holding him up to a mirror. From about three months, a baby might like to look at reflections.

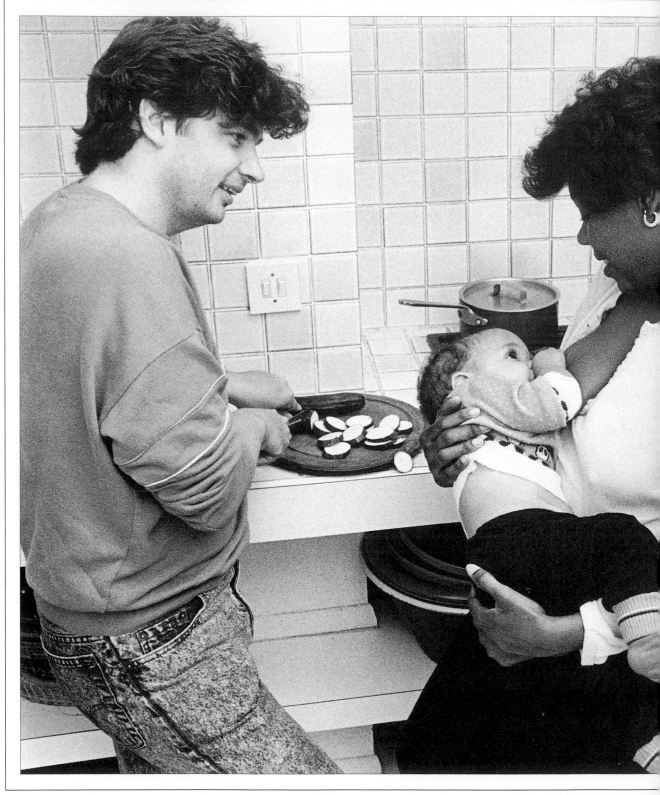

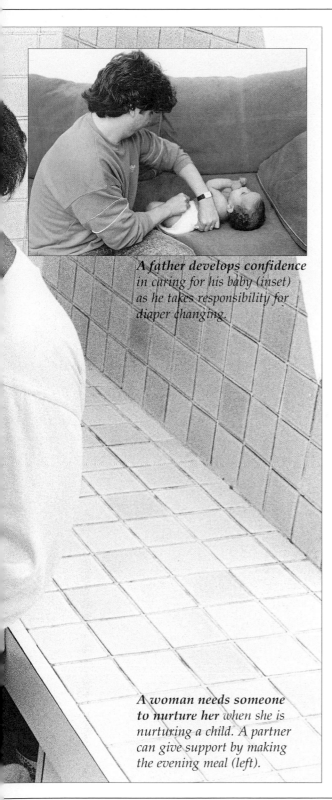

A father develops confidence in caring for his baby (inset) as he takes responsibility for diaper changing.

A woman needs someone to nurture her when she is nurturing a child. A partner can give support by making the evening meal (left).

A FATHER'S ROLE

Breastfeeding should in no way make a father feel superfluous. A woman who is nurturing a baby needs to be nurtured herself, and her partner may be the person who can do this best. There are many other things a baby needs beside feeding—to be held up to a mirror and smiled at; to be changed, bathed, and comforted; to be bounced, patted, rocked, and talked to. There are extra jobs to be done, too, including laundry, cooking, and shopping. Shared parenting means that a father takes on all these tasks. It is hard work but can be an enriching experience. In the first eight weeks, as your baby makes his postbirth adjustments, take a nap every day. A partner can see that this happens, even if it is only sleeping late in the morning or going to bed early in the evening.

When friends and relatives visit, enlist their help, too. Let them admire the baby. Then ask them to do something to help while you feed. You do not have to entertain them as before.

TIME FOR PLAY

If you do not have any help, you will find that you have little time for talking to, singing to, or playing with your baby, nor for providing stimulating things for her to explore with her senses. When you do these things you introduce a child to life with its richly varied experiences. You enable a baby to develop into a human being. A woman alone has little time to spare for this. Neither does a woman with older children at home, who may have her whole day filled with caring for, feeding, cleaning, and tidying up after them.

Other cultures organize child care better. There are comothers to share child care, and members of the extended family to take responsibility. In an industrialized society mothers must often bear total responsibility for their children, and may be socially isolated in what is virtually solitary confinement. Meanwhile, fathers often miss out on the early months of their children's lives, not just because they are away from home but also because mothers are expected to know instinctively how to care for babies, and men don't know how much they are needed.

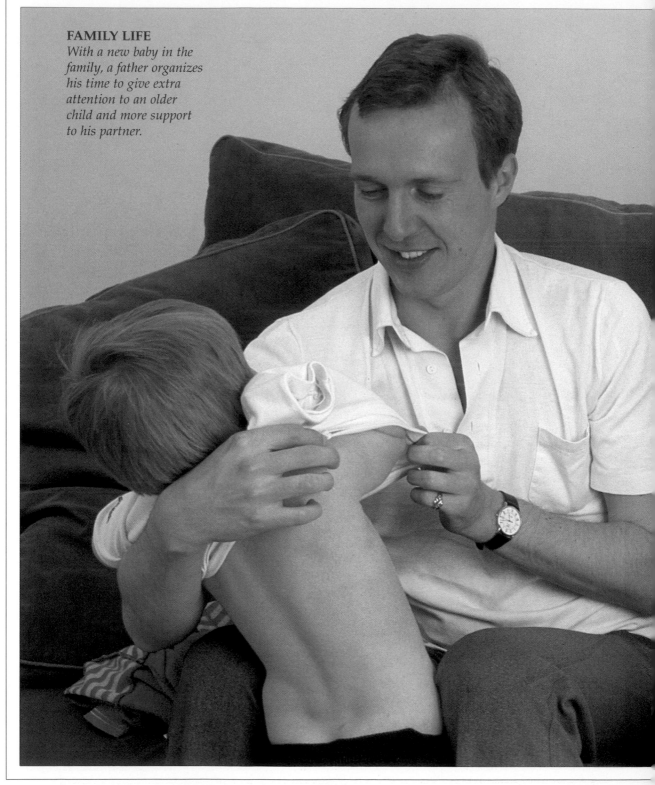

FAMILY LIFE
With a new baby in the family, a father organizes his time to give extra attention to an older child and more support to his partner.

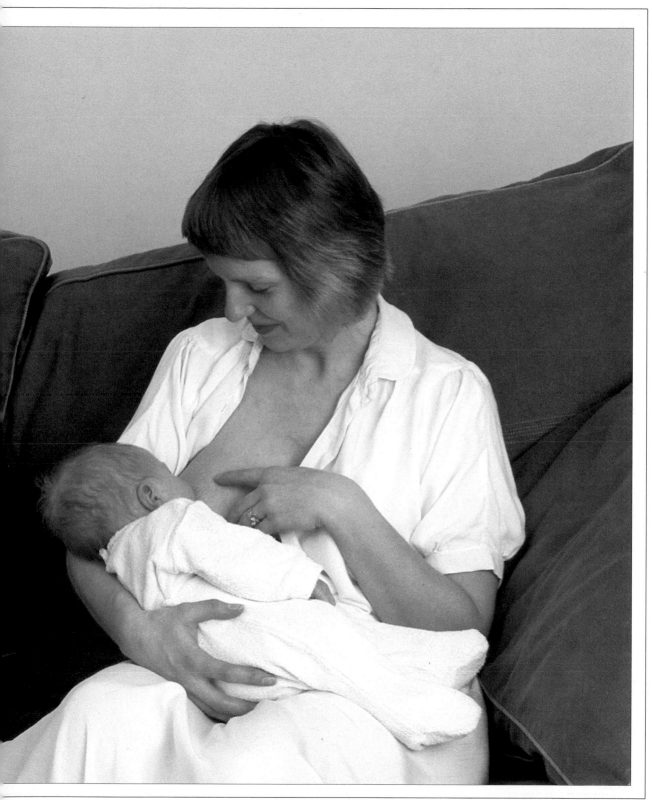

Your Needs

While keeping attuned to the baby's needs, it is important that you also be aware of your own needs. Most of the time the needs of a mother and her breastfed baby overlap. The baby comes to the breast and the mother feels the warmth and prickling rush of the milk ejection reflex, and has satisfaction in holding the baby and knowing that he is receiving milk. Yet sometimes a mother needs space to be herself, apart from the baby.

CONFIDENCE IN YOURSELF

A woman who is breastfeeding needs, above all, confidence in herself. She needs to feel in control. It helps to have support from other people around you—your family and friends, people who also believe that you can nurture your child and do not criticize you or undermine your faith in yourself. Those who give support should not try to take over the baby and replace you, or in any way compete for the baby's love. They are there ready to help when you need it, but respect the bond that links a mother and her baby, and realize that you will grow to understand each other.

A little advice goes a very long way. In fact, advice is often wrong; even if the facts are right, it can be destructive, and your attempts to follow it can distort the subtle relationship you have with your baby. New mothers can be bombarded with advice about how they could organize their lives better with the new baby (see page 51), especially from their own mothers. They worry that the baby is too demanding; they worry when he cries and want to say or do something to help. They may say and do the wrong things and leave you feeling like a failure. But if you follow your own instincts, you will be doing what is right for your baby and so naturally, your self-confidence will grow.

TIME FOR YOURSELF

A woman may need some regular time, however short, away from the baby. Much depends upon the birth experience. If this was good, and she emerged feeling strong and in control, she can

When a woman enjoys the other members of the family (below) and shares experiences with other women (inset), she can relax from her never-ending nurturing task.

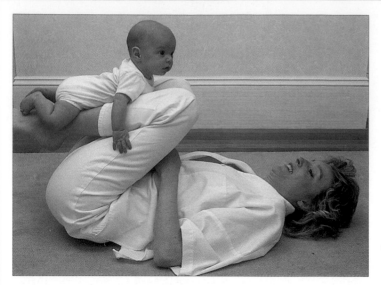

Exercises to tone your muscles can be done so that your baby enjoys them too (left). With the small of your back pressed flat against the floor, lay your baby along your shins and swing him on your legs to strengthen your tummy muscles.

relate to the baby and get "in tune" from the very beginning. She may feel vibrant with new energy and suffused with joy.

If, on the other hand, she feels in any way disempowered by what she has been through, she needs both uninterrupted time alone with her baby and space to be by herself without any demands being made on her. The timing of this is a matter for sensitive adjustment in the pattern of baby care through the 24 hours. It is vital for her to make time for herself wherever she can, rather than wearing herself out struggling to be a "good" mother. In order to do this, she needs another adult able and willing to take over everyday chores for her.

CHANGE OF ENVIRONMENT

Any woman with a baby or toddler benefits from a regular change in her environment, too. In one sense, a breastfeeding mother is in bondage to her baby, linked in mind and body and through her endocrine system and all the complex emotions she has about her baby. Much of this bondage is pleasurable, but for all of us there come times when we need to escape from the intensity and the demanding nature of this experience; we need to talk to adults, for example, or do something entirely different.

Many women are deprived of this opportunity, especially in the first year of a child's life,

because Western industrial societies are not organized for mothers and babies. Thousands of women with children are also caught in a poverty trap and are forced to use all their resources just to keep going from day to day.

If this is how it is for you, and there is a chance to get out of the house regularly, grab it. Whenever you can escape into the fresh air for a change of scene, do not hesitate to do so. Many women say that even a walk to the store, in spite of bad weather, or just chatting with other mothers while waiting at the school entrance, brings relief from the unremitting hard work and intense concentration that caring for a baby entails.

In good weather take a stroll in the park, or arrange a picnic with other mothers and children or a trip together to a swimming pool, into the countryside, or to the beach. Even meeting up with a friend in the shopping center can make a difference. You have the advantage as a breastfeeding mother of being able to feed your baby wherever you are. All you have to do is find somewhere to sit, open up, and let the baby latch on while you relax and enjoy the change of scene.

When you share with each other and do things you enjoy, you realize that you are not alone, that other women feel as you do, and that by joining together you are stronger and have much more confidence in yourselves.

A woman can cope best with the challenges of motherhood when she is part of a network of women with children (above and right) who are honest and open about their negative as well as their positive feelings, and who give each other emotional support and reassurance.

Fitting In with the Family

When your baby is born, your older child may feel replaced and rejected. She needs to know that you still love her and that you are not cutting short your time with her because of the new baby. You can prepare your other children by discussing the birth and breastfeeding well before the baby comes, and by showing them pictures of babies being born and at their mother's breast. If you have to change sleeping arrangements or routines, or want older children to be toilet-trained or to start playgroup, nursery, or school, do this several months before the baby comes or leave it until six months or so after the birth, to allow your child to settle down again.

SIBLING JEALOUSY

When you are breastfeeding you may find that an older child wants to suck, too, and to be held and cuddled. Sometimes children pretend they are babies again for a while. Rather than pushing them to "act their age," go along with this as if it were a pleasant game. By responding positively to your children's need of you, and by assuring them of your love, you will help them to feel secure.

An older child may prove very demanding when you have a baby at the breast, asking for a drink of water, doing things that are dangerous or very noisy, or even throwing a tantrum. Plan for this is advance. You can make sure that the room is completely safe and prepare your child's favorite drink or snack beforehand.

Once you have the baby well latched on, you can cuddle an older child, tell a story, or sing together, so that breastfeeding gives you all a special closeness. If you usually breastfeed in one room, keep a store of playthings there. The older child will know that when the baby is at the breast it is a sign to open that particular toy chest. Sibling jealousy is normal, but there are many ways in which you can help your child grow through this phase.

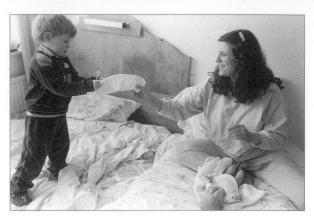

A HELPFUL TODDLER

1 *A young child helps by fetching things for the baby. His mother lets him know that she appreciates this.*

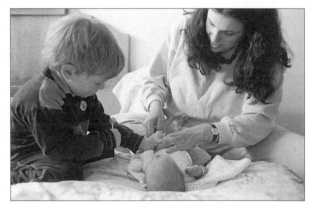

2 *He holds a diaper in place around the wriggling baby. By collaborating in this task, he learns a caring gentleness.*

3 *When he is given the responsibility of looking after the baby, he pats her gently and is delighted when she gazes up at him.*

4 With the baby dressed, the mother gives her son a warm hug, and tells him what a help he is.

THE NEEDS OF AN OLDER CHILD

1 *When you are concentrating on caring for the new baby, your other child may feel left out. Be sensitive to her feelings. There is no room in your arms for her and she is bereft, especially when there are twins.*

2 *When there is another adult you can trust, who gives extra love and attention to the older child, this helps her feel more secure. Instead of feeling that she has been usurped, she begins to enjoy the new additions to the family.*

Children develop nurturing abilities by the time they are five or six years old, and they like to help care for the new baby—and for their mother when she is focusing on his needs.

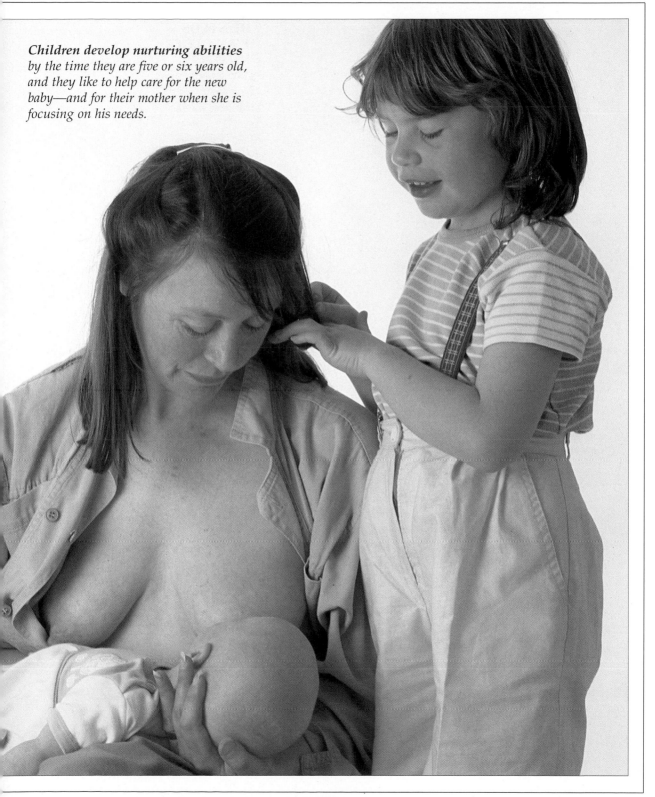

"I Should Have Stuck to Goldfish!"

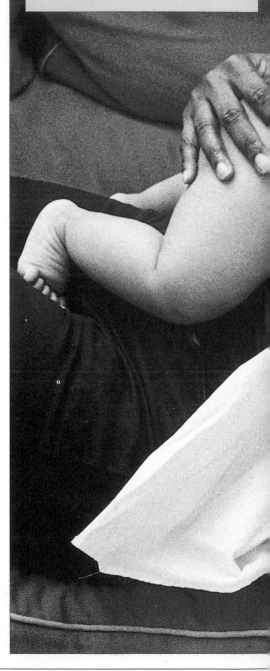

When she is upset, your baby may like to lie against you, warm and enfolded. Listen to soft music so you can relax and let peace flow through your body into the baby.

When a baby cries and fusses and demands all of your time, attention, and energy, you may feel like dumping him in the wastepaper basket. You are not the only mother who feels like this. Others do too—even apparently calm, happy, competent mothers. If you have had nothing to do with babies before, and your only experience of looking after anything was caring for your pet kitten or puppy or an even less demanding creature like a goldfish, there will probably be times when you wish you had never taken on the responsibility for this unreasonable, demanding, noisy, angry little baby. You don't have to put on an act!

THE FRETTING TIME

The evening is when it all starts for many babies. They become restless and cross, and nothing keeps them happy for more than a few minutes. One mother calls the period from six to seven p.m. "the arsenic hour." She is lucky—some babies go on fussing much longer. By that time of day you are ready to slow down and have a rest. You look forward to a quiet meal with your partner. But it is not to be.

Most babies who are past the immediate newborn stage and are not yet three or four months old have an irritable spell at some time in the day, when they want frequent feeds and like to return to the first breast after they have had a long session at both sides already. You then put them down to sleep, and they are awake again within half an hour, ready to feed.

You may wonder whether you have enough milk to satisfy your baby. However, this fretting time is nothing to do with either the quantity or the quality of your milk. It is rather that the baby is supercharged and in a state of nervous excitability in which he needs to discharge some tension by twitching, crying, jerking, wriggling, squirming, sucking, and treating you as if you were failing as a mother.

OFFERING DISTRACTIONS

Any and everything you do to try and help your baby may seem wrong. Some things work for a short while: more interesting surroundings, something that catches his attention, such as looking at himself in a mirror, gazing at a ticking clock, or watching older children playing. Soothing music sometimes helps, but the baby may be crying so

loudly that he cannot hear it. Carrying him around in a sling may be effective for longer still, especially if you keep moving. You may also find that it helps to lie down in a darkened room with the baby lying spread-eagled on your body, where he can hear the beating of your heart and feel the comforting warmth of your flesh. Or you could try simply rocking your baby and gently patting his back.

Placing a baby in a warm bath is a good way of helping him to relax, so it is sensible to plan bath time for that time of the day or evening when you know your baby is most likely to be in this restless state.

Another effective way of soothing a baby whose desperate crying is already reduced to sobs is to rest your head against his and to hum or intone so that the baby not only hears the sound of your voice but also feels the resonance. A deep, low tone is often best, but you can vary it. As the baby relaxes, your gentle reverberating hum can turn into singing—any sort of nonsense will do. Finding a way to soothe your baby is a matter of trial and error, always letting him lead the way. It can take weeks to discover what works best.

DETERMINED TO CRY

But then, just when you think that you have found an answer to his distress, you do something else that starts him crying again. You move and he is startled. You speak and he grimaces. You change position to try to get him more comfortable and he flinches and then yells even louder. It may seem impossible to know what to do to help your baby. He won't settle with you, and yet if you leave him alone he cries as if totally abandoned, and that is agony for you, too. There seems to be no answer.

Someone may tell you to put him in his crib and let him cry himself to sleep. But if you dump a frantically screaming baby in a crib, he is likely to cry more. He will fall asleep eventually, when exhausted, but he really needs to be calm before he can sleep peacefully.

THE BABY SLEEPS

At last the baby falls asleep and you breathe a sigh of relief. All is quiet for 15 or 20 minutes—an hour if you are lucky. Then the baby makes a convulsive movement and starts to cry irritably again. If you respond quickly, pat his bottom and offer a reassuring presence, he may drift back to sleep. Or it may be obvious that he is too upset for this and wants the comfort of the breast. Pick him up before he is in a full spate of crying, soothe him, and offer the breast; he may at last suck rhythmically, relax, and drop off to sleep.

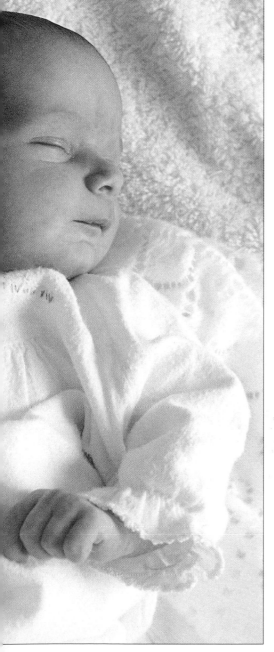

AN UNSETTLED BABY

1 *There are bound to be times when your baby is restless and fretful. She starts to twitch and toss and turn as if having a bad dream.*

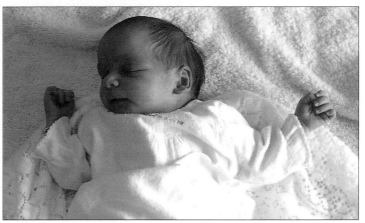

2 *She makes little jerky movements and wriggles, unable to settle. You watch her anxiously.*

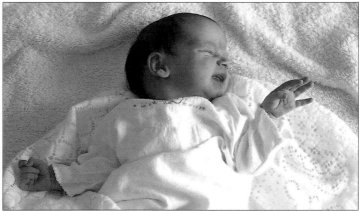

3 *Perhaps if you ignore her, she will settle. Other people tell you to put her in another room.*

4 *But you can't bear knowing that she is uncomfortable. She starts to cry. You pick her up.*

REASSURING YOUR BABY

1 *When your baby is crotchety, let him know you care by holding and talking to him and helping him feel secure in your arms.*

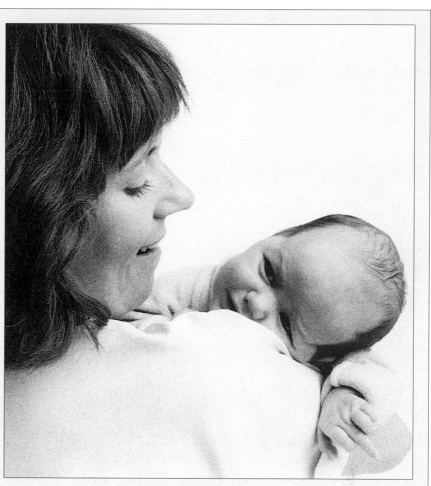

2 *It doesn't matter what nonsense you say, or what silly sounds you make. Do what comes spontaneously. The baby will know you are telling him that you love him.*

CALMING A CRYING BABY

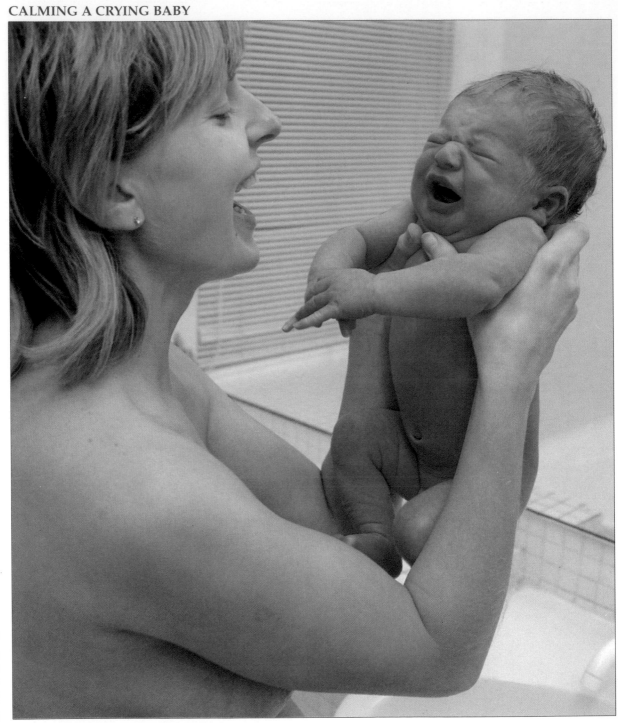

1 *A cranky baby can often be comforted by a warm bath, especially if you bathe together in a room where the ambient temperature is cozy for the baby.*

2 *Lie in a warm bath with the baby and cuddle together as you relax in the water. You can dim the lights to soothe him.*

3 *Support your baby's head and shoulders as he floats facing you so that you can gaze into each other's eyes and he can watch you smile and talk.*

4 *Afterward wrap your baby up in a big warm towel, give him an aromatherapy massage if he enjoys it, and offer the breast.*

THE PLEASURES OF THE BATH

If you don't mind having a lukewarm bath and have a pleasantly warm bathroom, you may enjoy taking your baby with you into your bath. And if you like music and candlelight, it may be that your baby will like these, too.

You can massage your baby with just a little relaxing aromatherapy oil while in the warm water. While you hold him, he can try out floating and kicking and you can invent little games. And, of course, you can breastfeed while you are still in the water.

Keep the air temperature warm and have big, thick bath towels to wrap yourselves up in afterward, as a wet baby quickly gets chilled.

A newborn baby will enjoy the sensation of floating and weightlessness, perhaps reliving the experience of lying in amniotic fluid inside your uterus. Little hands and feet will explore the water, because it is easy to move in it. An older baby will enjoy splashing, seeing the startled expression on your face, and hearing your laughter as you respond to this. Older still, the baby will discover how to splash you as part of a mutual splashing game. Having a bath can be a wet business!

An unhurried bath session like this can often unwind you both so that you are relaxed and ready for a breastfeed, and both you and the baby sleep deeply afterward.

A Developing Relationship

From birth onward, a mother and her baby imitate each other. They are joined together in a kind of dance. The baby makes a certain face, pouting her lips forward perhaps, or opening her mouth wide, and the mother unconsciously copies it. Then she raises her eyebrows, purses her lips and sticks out her tongue. After a pause, the baby may do so too in unconscious imitation.

Babies hear very well from the beginning of life, and have a strong preference for speech sounds. As you talk to your baby, her muscles contract and relax in response to your speech. She is tuned to the frequencies of your voice and the language you speak. She learns your speech patterns with her body, and they become part of her.

AT ONE MONTH

When only a few weeks old, your baby may often look as if she is about to burst into speech. By about one month old she can have a well-organized "conversation" with you. It may be gossipy, witty, or sad, depending on her mood. In another month you may notice that, as you talk to her, she sometimes molds her lips and tongue into the shapes that will later make the sounds of speech, and waves her hands about as she tells you all about it, as if she were an adult having an enthusiastic discussion. Take it at a slow pace, and wait patiently for the responses.

AT TWO MONTHS

By the time your baby is six to eight weeks old, you will be aware of different, contrasting aspects of her character. Sometimes when she half wakes, hungry for a feed, she is like a little animal groping for the breast, with her fists clenched, eyes tightly shut, mouth open and rooting, and the cry as plaintive as that of a newborn lamb. She is simply a baby. She might be anybody's baby, and not even one whom you like particularly. You don't feel you really know her as an individual with a personality.

At other times, when your baby is alert and wide-eyed, she seems to be much older. When she wants to feed, it is as if she is telling you what she wants and even asking for the breast. It is almost as if she is talking to you. The baby is now a person, unique and special, with whom you can communicate.

This swing between a baby's yearning need—a being with a gaping mouth, closed eyes, and a body rigid with desire—and her development as a little person who makes you smile and laugh and feel good about her and yourself often continues until she is about three or four months old and sometimes longer.

THE CHARACTER EMERGES

Over the following weeks the baby's individual identity and strong character will become more obvious and you will get to know her more and more as a person. She may start to pat, stroke, or push your breast with her hand, which is now sometimes opened up rather than curled into a fist. She looks up at you and stares into your eyes. She nibbles or bites you and smiles. Sometimes she protests about something she does not like in a cross voice, pushing her lower lip out as if feeling sorry for herself. When she is contented, she coos, and occasionally the inflections in her voice sound as if she is talking.

ENJOYING YOUR BABY

The times when the baby is relating to you and is alert and interested in her surroundings grow longer and longer. You can begin to enjoy your baby in new ways, and in return, your baby enjoys you—drawing your attention toward what she wants you to notice, responding to you, and joining in games. She stands facing you on your lap and jumps with a delighted sense of achievement. She concentrates on bold pictures in a book, held for her so that she can rub them and discover with surprise that she cannot pick objects up off the page. When she wakes she will lie contented for a while, knowing that a feed is coming, playing with her toes or fingers or a rattle, or gazing, fascinated, at a mobile.

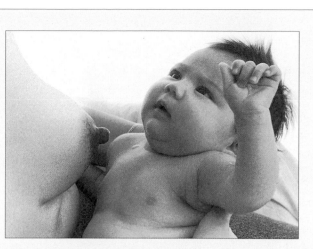

A baby is completely absorbed by her mother's face, watching her lips move as she talks to her and looking up into her eyes as she is moved to the breast (inset).

It is never too early to start reading to a baby. Cloth books are more or less indestructible and, in primary colors, they fascinate a baby. You can make up your own stories to fit the pictures. Your baby will try to pick the pictures up off the pages, and will even try chewing on the book to see if it tastes good, too.

This is the time when, no longer having to provide a split-second response to your baby's need for you, you can reclaim a little space and relax in the knowledge that, in spite of your doubts, you are a good enough mother and can enjoy a new freedom.

AT THREE MONTHS

By the time your baby is ten to twelve weeks old, she will already have definite ways of letting you know what she wants. If you put her to the breast and she does not wish to be fed, she may go rigid, arch her back, throw up her arms, and protest loudly. Or she may take the opportunity to play with your breasts if she is in the mood. Breasts are splendid playthings because they are soft and bouncy. She may lick the nipple or tickle it with her lips, try to chew it, or even grab and bite you—all the time watching you. She finds your reactions very interesting. When she is rough with you, withdraw and tell her quite firmly that she must not do it again as you do not like it. She will soon understand.

WAKE AND SLEEP STATES

When your baby wakes but is still groggy with sleep, she may shift into a more comfortable position. If she is prone, she may stick her bottom in the air and creep forward with a kind of caterpillar propulsion until she has her head resting against something firm—the top of the crib or a wall or cupboard—and then close her eyes again and have another snooze. If you pick her up before she has had this extra sleep she may be very irritable because she was not ready to wake up.

A baby who has had a good sleep may wake refreshed and want simply to be assured of your presence. Then she starts to explore the surroundings and to play. She waves her fist in the air and watches it with close, cross-eyed concentration. She brings her hands together, and each gropes for the other, but often misses, and they go right past each other She kicks, finds a foot with her hand, holds it for an exciting moment, and then loses it again. If a mirror is set alongside her, she will turn and watch the other baby with great seriousness. Then she chuckles.

Some babies are sociable *(above), while others are more thoughtful and contemplative (below). As they develop, outgoing babies become quiet if they have interesting things to explore. Placid babies become sociable when with a trusted person.*

When in an exuberant mood the baby talks to anyone and anything around—a picture on the wall, a chair, and herself—with little whoops and chortles of delight. If she gets bored, this conversation becomes querulous and there is a note of impending trouble. When you are busy with something else and half listening to her, you know immediately that she is ready for a different occupation.

A baby likes anything hanging on a string or ribbon—a mobile, a balloon, a leafy branch, a jingling necklace, or a bell—that can be swiped at with hands or feet. You can make simple homemade mobiles and suspend them from a wire coathanger over the back of a chair. Your baby will try to get everything into her mouth to explore it fully, so it is vital that there is nothing on which she can choke or that can scratch or bruise her.

UNDERSTANDING YOUR BABY

There are times when the baby seems to be furious with you for no reason. She cries at the top of her voice and whatever you do is wrong.

Other people ask, "Is she hungry? . . . Too hot? . . . Too cold? . . . Have you changed her diaper?" It makes you feel inept and guilty that you might be a bad mother, and sometimes even desperate. And then suddenly, as you cuddle her close, all her anger vanishes.

But after a while she starts to cry again. You know your baby well enough by now to realize that these are signs that she is overtired and that even if you are not successful at comforting her, the message that you are trying to give comfort is important. Eventually the cries become sobs and you are able to soothe her to sleep.

A baby may also be restless because she is about to empty her bowels and is concentrating on something inside her that disturbs her. Then, with an expression of intense satisfaction, she holds her breath, grunts, and you hear the unmistakable sounds of a stool being passed.

Over the last weeks you have watched your baby carefully and you know, as no one else quite understands, all these very different emotional and physical states. You understand your baby as a unique individual.

RHYTHMS OF A BABY

1 By four months your baby is happy to lie and play by herself for a while when she wakes (right). She takes great delight in discovering her own foot and is in no hurry to feed. You hear gurgles, coos, and squeals as she experiments with sounds.

2 *When she is ready for a feed, she lets you know with an urgent cry. She knows exactly how to latch on and sucks with relish (left). Her initial excitement gives way to blissful relaxation.*

3 *After being awake for a few hours she becomes tearful (right). You know she must be overtired and needs to be soothed so that she can go to sleep. But she finds it difficult to relax and is not easily*

4 *Eventually you are able to soothe her off to sleep (right). She sleeps soundly, even though there may be noise all around her. And when she wakes afresh, she will be bursting with renewed energy.*

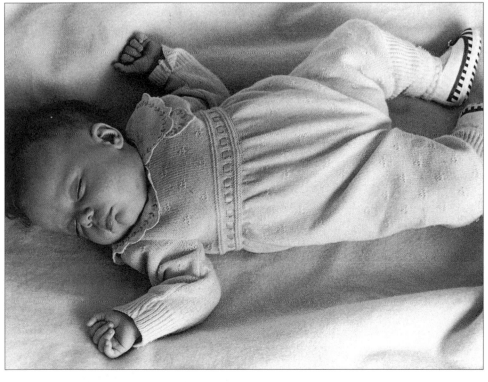

SECURITY AND ADVENTURE

The Older Baby

AS YOUR BABY DEVELOPS, feeding becomes fun for you both. It is like a lively conversation with lots of eye contact, smiles, giggles, and gurgles. Your baby may murmur and talk to you, too, imitating the cadences of your own speech, stopping so that you can have a turn, and then replying.

THE EXPERIENCED FEEDER

An older baby knows exactly where the breast is and homes in on it through layers of clothing with unerring aim. He may indicate that you should lift your sweater or undo your shirt, and then discover that he can do this himself. He may become adept at shifting clothing and, later still, at undoing buttons, snaps, and zippers. This is the stage at which you may find your breasts suddenly bared in public!

Some babies experiment with acrobatic feeds. They like exploring the effect of different positions. Once fully mobile, a baby who is an expert feeder may latch on to a handy breast from any angle. He may crawl right up to you and feed while still leaning against your body.

An older baby often comes into contact with other children. By continuing to breastfeed your baby, you are providing the anti-infective properties of breastmilk, making him less likely to get colds, tummy upsets, and earaches. If your baby does catch a cold, it tends to be less severe than that of a baby fed with formula.*

TEETHING

When the first tooth is about to come through, your baby's gum may be sore and he likes to gnaw and bite. He may want to suck at the breast for comfort, but if he tries to bite you, take him off firmly and say "No." He will soon understand. Help your baby's teething by giving him objects to bite on such as a teething ring, zwieback, or a rattle of convenient size. You can give him easily grasped pieces of raw carrot or apple, but watch over him in case he chokes. Some teething rings can be filled with water and then frozen.

ATTITUDES OF OTHER PEOPLE

Other people may disapprove if you breastfeed your toddler. In Western society great emphasis is laid on babies progressing quickly toward independence. People are often fearful that any prolonged breastfeeding—into the second year of life and beyond—ties the baby to the mother. In fact, the opposite is true. A child who is secure and confident of love, and who knows that the mother is close at hand, is better able to make explorations away from her. So if you can, continue breastfeeding as long as your baby wants it, and let him decide when to stop.

If you are sitting on the ground, *your toddler may make a beeline for your breast and feed leaning against you.*

An older child invents games at the breast, unbuttoning and unzipping you, stroking your hair and pretending to capture your nose.

Expressing Milk

It is useful to be able to express your breastmilk so that if you are away from your baby, someone else can give her a bottle. If your breasts become engorged and uncomfortable, expressing milk will relieve them. There are several ways to express milk. Whichever method you use, have a clean towel handy to mop up any spills. If you intend to keep the milk, wash your hands first and be sure that any equipment you use is sterilized. Store the milk in the refrigerator or freezer.

To stimulate your milk ejection reflex, rest a hot towel or heating pad against your breast. Then cup your breast with one hand and with the other hand gently massage it, stroking from the outer edges in toward the nipple, all the way around as if following the spokes of a wheel. Or use a comb that you have drawn through soft soap (leave a cake of soap in a wet dish) sweeping the comb from the outer margins of the breast in toward the areola.

GRAVITY FLOW

The simplest method of expressing milk is to lean forward so that your breasts hang down and then exert gentle pressure with your hands. This works well if you have a great deal of milk and a good milk ejection reflex. It may be the easiest way of releasing milk if your breasts feel very full, and if you just want to achieve a softer breast for the baby.

HAND EXPRESSION

Hand expression is a simple technique when you know how. After massaging your breast, lean forward, supporting your breast underneath with three fingers of one hand, and put the index finger of the other hand below the lower edge of the areola and your thumb above its upper edge. Relax your shoulder and neck muscles and try to breathe slowly. Then gently and rhythmically squeeze the breast, as if you were squeezing toothpaste from a tube. To get the maximum amount of milk, move your fingers and thumb around the outside of your breast, as if traveling

USING A NIPPLE SHIELD

1 *To collect dripping milk while you feed, put a nipple shield inside you nursing bra. Hook up the bra to keep the shield in place.*

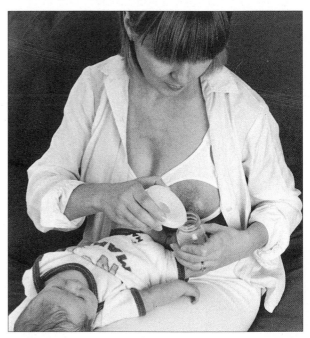

2 *When you can feel that it is almost full, remove it carefully and decant it into a jar for storage in the refrigerator or freezer.*

EXPRESSING MILK BY HAND

1 *To start the milk flow, support your breast with one hand and massage it with the other (right). Stroke down from your armpit toward the areola and then all around the globe of the breast.*

2 *Squeeze the lower part of the breast rhythmically with your thumb and index finger (below), pressing deeply in on the glandular tissue to force the milk down.*

3 *Drops of milk glisten on the nipple and then milk spurts out in a steady stream (below right). Keep the flow going by gradually moving your hand around the outer edge of the areola.*

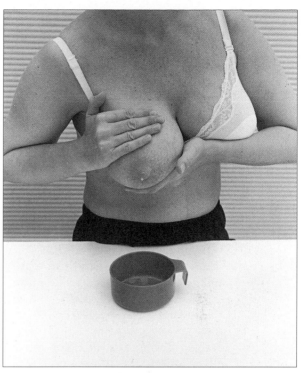

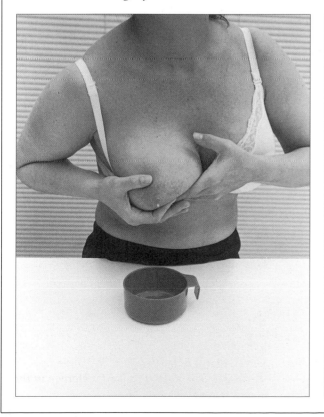

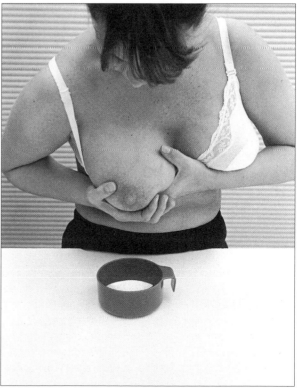

around the numbers on a clock face. This frees the milk ducts and avoids blockage of milk and inflammation. Many women can express milk without a breast pump—so you don't have to be dependent on a pump.*

USING A HAND PUMP

Hand pumps use a piston movement from a syringe or a trigger action from a lever to produce suction on the breast. Hand pumps can be quicker and easier than hand expression, and you may get more efficient milking of the breast.

EXPRESSING WITH A HAND PUMP

USING AN ELECTRIC BREAST PUMP

An electric pump is most efficient—almost as efficient as a baby. Start the pump on its minimum suction setting, or the pull can be painful. As you get used to the sensation, gradually increase the suction. If your baby is in special care you will need to use the pump every two to three hours. It helps to make a definite routine for this. This may be difficult to do at home if you are under pressure to cook, clean, and run the house, especially if you have other children. If possible, arrange for other people to take over chores.

1 *Use a sterilized pump to express your milk. Wash your equipment thoroughly in soapy water, rinse it well, and submerge it in a special sterilizing solution for at least 30 minutes. Many pumps are sold with sealed containers for this.*

2 *Pour the expressed breastmilk from the pump into a sterilized bottle or a plastic bag that fits inside a bottle. Seal it and label it with the date and any other information you want to record for future reference.*

3 *Place the milk in the freezer, where it will keep for up to six months. Or you can put it in the refrigerator—not in the door, as the temperature there is warmer—for use within 24 hours.*

4 *Thaw the frozen milk by holding it under a hot tap. Then stand it in hot water to warm it. The milk will have separated, but this does not matter. Use defrosted milk within a few hours.*

Types of Breast Pumps

When using a breast pump, treat your breasts gently and do not rush pumping, or you may cause nipple damage. Find a place where you have some privacy. Relax as you pump. Have a drink or a snack and read, or listen to music. Reading an article on breastfeeding, or this book, and looking at attractive pictures of mothers and babies breastfeeding will help your milk ejection reflex. When you are at work, a regular routine of pumping helps you produce plenty of milk and avoids milk stasis and the pain that results from blocked ducts. Portable kits are convenient, providing spare bottles and a cooler bag. Tie in pumping sessions with your usual breaks.

Manual breast pumps
If you can choose from a varied selection, consider how each pump may be appropriate for you (right). Feel the weight and look at the size of the nipple shield. Many pumps also have adjustable suction strength. The suitability of each pump will depend upon how easy it is for you to use. (See also page 164.)

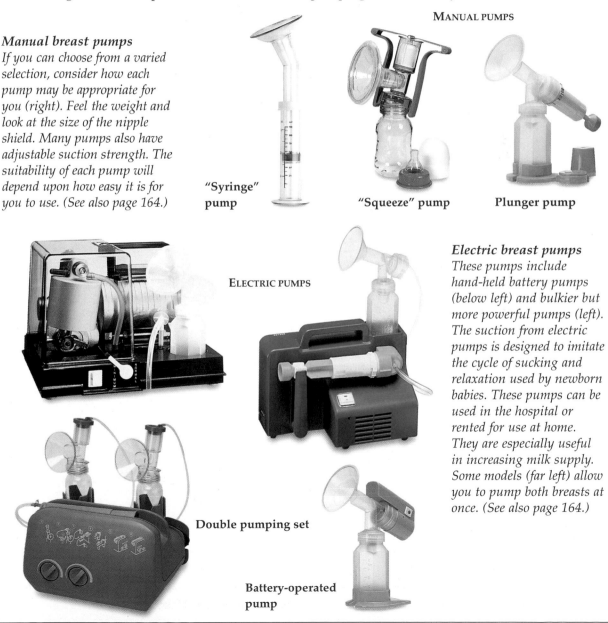

MANUAL PUMPS

"Syringe" pump

"Squeeze" pump

Plunger pump

ELECTRIC PUMPS

Double pumping set

Battery-operated pump

Electric breast pumps
These pumps include hand-held battery pumps (below left) and bulkier but more powerful pumps (left). The suction from electric pumps is designed to imitate the cycle of sucking and relaxation used by newborn babies. These pumps can be used in the hospital or rented for use at home. They are especially useful in increasing milk supply. Some models (far left) allow you to pump both breasts at once. (See also page 164.)

Sex and Breastfeeding

After you have had your baby you may be aching to get back to "normal" as soon as possible; on the other hand, you may enjoy the different way your body feels and looks. Breastfeeding, and your confidence about it, will affect how you think about your body.

THE PLEASURE OF BREASTFEEDING

Some women find that breastfeeding is simply a nurturing task, though a satisfying one, and gives a closeness to the baby that helps them to get to know him.

Other women discover—occasionally to their surprise—that breastfeeding is an elating experience. It brings to their bodies a delicious sensitivity, as well as a feeling of fulfillment. A woman who relishes breastfeeding may feel sexually aroused as her baby tugs and sucks. These feelings make some women feel ashamed and guilty. Yet it is normal to feel intense physical pleasure in breastfeeding, and sometimes even to have an orgasm as a result.

Most of us probably experience both these feelings at different times. We veer between simply managing to fit breastfeeds into our busy lives and experiencing them as deeply satisfying and even blissful.

FEELINGS ABOUT SEX

In the early weeks—and sometimes months—of breastfeeding, many women are not sexually aroused in a way they have been previously, and do not enjoy genital sex. This is understandable. If you are facing difficulties in breastfeeding, you probably do not feel at all good about your body and think of it as cumbersome and awkward. This, in turn, affects how you feel about sex. When you are trying to cope with breastfeeding problems, you are likely to be anxious about them, and there is little time or energy left over for erotic sexual feelings.

For some women this reduction of libido persists right through the time they are lactating, probably as a result of the hormones that

stimulate milk production. Your partner should be aware that when you know your baby is about to wake for a feed and you are listening for the first cry, or if you are worrying about the baby, you cannot concentrate on lovemaking. Without this mental focus, any sexually arousing experience is just physical. Intense sexual excitement comes only when mind and body together have the same strong focus.

In the first weeks after childbirth you may be going through physical changes that cause pain or discomfort. An episiotomy wound and suturing of the perineum, heavy blood loss, and physical exhaustion can all result in feeling that the last thing you want to think about at this time, or ever again, is sex.

However much you enjoy being a mother, your new role is bound to be stressful, too. There are all sorts of things to learn and challenges to confront. Your whole way of life changes. The relationship between you and your partner evolves, with your baby an important part of it. Worrying about not feeling sexually aroused makes this transition more difficult. Take it one day at a time. If you had a good relationship before the baby came, you will find it again once you relax and the baby becomes part of the changing flow of your lives.

SEXUAL ABUSE

A woman who is a survivor of sexual abuse may find it hard to relax when breastfeeding. There are often flashbacks to abuse in which a man sucked or bit her breasts. For others who have been abused, breastfeeding proves empowering, since they are using their bodies in a positive way. Even a woman who starts off feeling that the baby is yet another person who is abusing her often starts to enjoy breastfeeding once it is going well.*

EFFECTS OF BREASTFEEDING

While you are breastfeeding you may notice that your vagina is especially dry, even when you are sexually aroused. This is because during lactation the level of estrogen circulating in your body is lower than usual. If you wish to have intercourse, use a lubricant that either you or your partner can stroke into the dry tissues—you can make this a pleasurable part of lovemaking. In the early weeks of breastfeeding your nipples may feel tender and sore, and nipple stimulation during lovemaking may hurt. Any pressure on your breasts may be painful while you are lactating, especially if they are full because a feed is due shortly. Your partner should avoid putting weight on your breasts or squeezing them during lovemaking. The "missionary" position for intercourse may be uncomfortable for this reason.

Babies have an uncanny sixth sense that seems to tell them when you are making love. They decide this is exactly the time they need to be fed; this is "baby interruptus," rather than coitus interruptus. The best time to enjoy leisurely lovemaking is immediately after a baby has settled following a feed.

EXPLORING NEW WAYS OF LOVEMAKING
You may often feel that you want to make love but not have intercourse. Lovemaking after childbirth enables you to explore together ways of arousing and satisfying each other that are far more complex and enriching than simple penetration and ejaculation. Some men who previously have ejaculated fast learn to prolong lovemaking so that it is much more satisfying for the woman, and in slowing down they become more gentle. A woman may discover she is capable of intense sexual arousal when all a partner is using is a little finger or a tenderly searching mouth.

A woman who is breastfeeding may feel that she doesn't want her partner making love to her breasts, even though she enjoyed it a great deal before the baby was born and will again when lactation is over. She feels that her breasts belong to the baby and finds it difficult to mix in her mind the sensations that her baby and her lover arouse. Or she may welcome her partner's touch, and be happy about drawing her partner to her breasts. But he may feel anxious about touching or sucking her breasts, and carefully avoid any

contact with them. The important thing is to be open about how you feel and recognize that there are no rules about how you should behave.

When you experience orgasm there is a sudden surge of oxytocin, the hormone that stimulates the milk ejection reflex. This pours into your bloodstream and milk may spurt from your breasts. This can feel very good. But some women hold back from reaching a climax because they dislike this involuntary milk ejection, or are aware that their partner dislikes it, and thinks of it as messy. The flow of milk during lovemaking is part of your body's richness and vitality in the same way that juices are released around your cervix and in your vagina, your whole body becomes hot and damp, and your eyes shine and your cheeks glow during intense sexual excitement.

However sex after birth turns out to be for you and your partner, whatever problems you confront, enjoy your baby together. Take this opportunity of new closeness to explore diverse ways of making love which give expression to your caring and tenderness for each other.

If you are exhausted, *you are unlikely to feel sexually aroused, and long for a stretch of blissful uninterrupted sleep.*

Breastfeeding with Confidence

In many countries women can breastfeed their babies unself-consciously wherever they are, and no one thinks twice about it. But in most Western industrialized countries mothers are supposed to make themselves invisible. Other people's raised eyebrows make it very difficult to breastfeed outside the home—when you are out shopping, or on a plane or train, or when you go out for a meal. Many women find that they are expected to breastfeed in the restroom. Unless you are very strong-minded and can cope with people's whispered remarks, rude stares, and icy requests that you go elsewhere, this may be the only place readily available.

OTHER PEOPLE'S REACTIONS
You may find the idea of breastfeeding in front of other people embarrassing because it is not usual for women to bare their breasts in public, unless they are bathing on a topless beach. Sometimes a partner, parents, or friends express distaste when a woman puts the baby to the breast at the dinner table or at a social gathering, because they feel there is something disgusting about breastfeeding or that a woman is flaunting herself sexually. Yet nurturing a baby is one of the most important commitments any human being can make. This is what breasts are for.

STAYING CALM AND SELF-ASSURED
If you wear clothing that is easily opened and have a big wrap or cape with you, you can breastfeed discreetly wherever you happen to be. Being with another woman who provides support—your mother, perhaps, or a friend—can give you extra courage, too, especially when you take your baby out the first few times.

When other people notice you breastfeeding, you can smile with the knowledge that you are doing the right thing. If anyone asks you to leave a shop or restaurant, politely refuse, saying, "No, I can't stop now. My baby's hungry and I have to

Wearing loose clothing makes feeding easier and more private if you are self-conscious. Then you can relax when you need to feed your baby outside the home, and concentrate on him.

feed her." If they tell you that a ladies' restroom is available for this, you can say, "No thank you. Would you like to eat *your* meal in a bathroom?" Then continue breastfeeding, just concentrating on your baby and her need of you. Your self-assurance may give other mothers the courage to do the same.

MAKING BREASTFEEDING MORE ACCEPTABLE
By letting others know you are breastfeeding, and breastfeeding openly, you help it become more acceptable for other women, too. When women in industrial countries take breastfeeding for granted, and do it with style, we give support to mothers and babies in Third World countries which are industrializing fast, and most of all to those where artificial feeding is for many babies a sentence of death.

If you join a breastfeeding organization (see page 164), you will meet other mothers who are facing the same challenges, and together you can develop ways of asserting your right—and the right of all women—to breastfeed openly.

When you are confident about breastfeeding in public, you can feed your baby whenever he is hungry (below). If you wear front-opening clothing, a convenient way to feed your baby is to have him cuddled up in a baby sling (inset).

Traveling

A breastfeeding mother has a distinct advantage over one who bottle-feeds. Milk is instantly available for her baby (in easily transported containers!), at the right temperature and free of harmful bacteria, whatever the climate or the surrounding environment.

A PLACE TO BREASTFEED
When you are away from home, the search for somewhere you can feed your baby may at first seem a daunting one. Rather than resorting to a ladies' room—not a hygenic arrangement— you may find a mother and baby room at airports and in some department stores. You can often also use first-aid rooms for feeding. A quiet corner in a restaurant or a changing cubicle in a dress shop may be suitable, or it may be worth asking in a pharmacy or children's store if there is somewhere you can sit and breastfeed. If it is a warm day, you can breastfeed on a park bench or under the trees on the grass. And almost everywhere you will be able to find a church or other place of worship in which you can feed in private. Breastfeeding on public transportation may be easier if you have a large shawl or scarf to throw over your shoulder. In a private car you can also drape this over the window so that it acts as a sunscreen as well as giving you a little privacy.

TRAVELING IN HOT WEATHER
When you are traveling in hot weather or are likely to become stressed by travel arrangements, make sure that you get sufficient fluids yourself. A mother who is dehydrated will not find it easy to calm a restless, thirsty baby, because her milk ejection reflex may be delayed. It may be a good idea to carry a carton of juice or bottle of water with you.

USEFUL ITEMS TO PACK
Always travel with a good supply of breastpads so that you do not stain your clothing. If your breasts leak it is also useful to have a spare towel to put under your top half as you lie in bed, so that you do not worry about staining the mattress.

FLYING WITH A BABY
On a plane, the stewardess may offer you a bottle for the baby and be rather surprised when you tell her you are feeding him yourself. She may offer to make up a bottle of water, at least, for the baby. Ask for a glass of water for yourself instead.

Takeoff and landing entail a change of air pressure inside the cabin and the baby will be more comfortable when this occurs if he either cries or sucks. So if he is awake, offer him the breast after takeoff and as the plane starts its descent to land.

CHANGE IN TEMPERATURE
If you are traveling somewhere hot, your baby may want more frequent feeds than at home, at least while he adjusts to the change in temperature. If he seems overheated, reverse the normal order of feeding: instead of offering the first breast again after an interval in sucking, offer him the other side, so that more dilute milk is available to quench his thirst.

Travel almost invariably entails disturbance for the baby, and the breast comforts and provides security in unfamiliar surroundings.

If you can take a shawl or blind to hang over the window you can park the car and breastfeed in privacy.

Going Back to Work

You can continue to breastfeed your baby after returning to work. You may be fortunate in having a nursery at work, or your workplace may be so close to home that you can return for feeds during breaks in your working time. However, few mothers are able to do this. Instead, pack your freezer with breastmilk, so that a caregiver can feed your baby at a moment's notice. The milk will keep in a freezer for up to six months. Start storing milk whenever you like—even early on, when the milk first comes in. But you may feel more confident about this after a few weeks when the supply is established. Many women are anxious that they will not have sufficient milk for their baby if they take some for freezing. In fact, demand creates supply, and you will produce more.

If you notice that milk is leaking when you are at work, press your elbows firmly against your breasts. This will slow down the milk flow. Wear breast pads to protect your clothing, and change them often so they don't become too damp.

STOCKPILING YOUR MILK

There are three ways to build a milk "larder." One is by collecting milk in a nipple shield from one breast while you feed from the other. It is easiest if you have a copious supply in the early weeks, and milk is spurting out from both sides as the baby sucks. After a while this settles down and you do not spurt or leak so much. Milk collected this way contains less fat than expressed breastmilk, as most of it is foremilk. The second method is to express milk at the end of a feed, either manually or with a pump. Or third, fit in an extra total expression session at a time of day, usually early in the morning or at night, when you have a copious supply.

Many women feel torn in two emotionally when they first have to split their lives between mothering and paid work. However, the sight of all those little containers full of your milk is encouraging and will make you feel more confident about going back to work.

KEEPING UP YOUR MILK SUPPLY

It helps to express milk during your working day, initially to avoid discomfort and possible engorgement, and later to keep up your milk supply as you get into a new lactational rhythm. Investigate quiet, clean, and private places where you can do this. You may get odd stares from some colleagues, who think that what you are doing is distasteful, and approval from others.

Keep equipment in sterilizing fluid in a plastic container. If there is a refrigerator, store milk in it as soon as it is expressed, or in a vacuum flask packed in ice. Otherwise, to throw it away, as it is risky to keep milk at room temperature.

If you cannot save milk during the day, express after the early-morning feed so that your baby can be fed while you are at work. But unless you have some in your freezer from earlier weeks, this milk may need topping up.

A baby has growth spurts during which she wants more milk. It is easy to interpret these as a sign that you no longer have enough milk, and you may lose confidence in your ability to breastfeed. The answer is to express milk more often when you are separated from your baby. This will stimulate your milk supply. Take extra time on the weekends for feeding. Go to bed if you can and try the 24-Hour Peak Production Plan (see page 106).

OTHER CULTURES

In many cultures, peasant women who work in the fields breastfeed into the second or third year of a child's life. The mother often works with her baby slung on her back or nestled against her hip. In Turkey, women pick cotton while their babies rock in cradles suspended from a wooden tripod, where the mothers can keep an eye on them. Other women help, too. A review of 186 nonindustrial cultures showed that mothers were exclusive caregivers in only five.* In many cultures the baby is left with an older woman, and other women, including a grandmother, will breastfeed if the baby needs it, while the mother works on the land. In some Israeli kibbutzim baby-minders fly a flag to tell the mother when to come in from the fields to feed her baby. It is difficult to adapt these methods to the modern work environment because the value of breastfeeding is not acknowledged. It is treated as a personal matter between a mother and her baby, not as important social policy.

WORK OPTIONS

Research shows that in any given year, 93 percent of babies fed on formula suffer illness compared with 59 percent of breastfed babies. This report stimulated some major American companies to facilitate breastfeeding in their workforce, on the premise that every dollar invested in providing breastfeeding facilities saved five dollars in absenteeism.* You may, however, find it hard to convince your managers that breastfeeding benefits business! The ideal solution for some women is to have extended maternity leave, and phase themselves back into work gradually. That means four to six months at home with the baby, a shorter working day for the rest of the first year, and a live-in trained nanny. This may prove impossible. But there are other options:

• More and more people are working part time at home, using fax, phone, and e-mail. This may suit you if you are self-disciplined and have on-the-spot child care. You are right there when your baby needs you. It may be possible if you work in an office, but obviously not if you have to be in direct contact with people.

• Flex-time may be the answer. Leave for work early, before the rush hour, or later in the morning, and come home before or after the rush hour. When the journey to and from work takes a long time, avoiding the rush-hour cuts wasted hours traveling every week.

• Perhaps you could drop your child off with a trusted caregiver, or a family member close to your place of work, so that you can use breaks and mealtimes to breastfeed. You run out to the baby-sitter's, or the baby can be brought to you.

• If there is no nursery in your place of work, get together with a group of mothers to organize one with a nursery nurse.

• Maybe you could alternate working in the office and working at home with your partner. He gives bottles of your expressed milk on your away-from-home days and you breastfeed and pump your milk on your at-home days.

• Or do a job share with someone else, perhaps someone who has older children and who understands the challenges you face, but is through that special phase of breastfeeding.

• Phase yourself into work as the baby gets older, starting with a few hours a week and building up to full time as you become more confident about child care.

• Or you may want to work part time until your child is older, doing just mornings, for example, so that you only miss one feed.

• Though choices may be limited, a woman today should not assume that if she returns to work she must give up breastfeeding. Combining work and breastfeeding entails planning, determination, and confidence, as well as having reliable support. But it can be done.

LOOKING AFTER YOURSELF

Combining motherhood and work outside the home is always difficult: mixing motherhood and work inside the home is hard enough.

Mothers are sitting targets for advice, much of which does not work (see page 51). Only you know your baby, the financial and other constraints that limit your options. But here are some suggestions:

• Do not attempt to keep too many balls in the air at once. Decide on priorities.

• Try not to skip meals. Eat breakfast. Avoid junk food. Have simple meals of cheese and salad.

• Make time to relax, whether it is to read a book, swim in the pool, get a massage, work out in the gym, take a break in the garden, or listen to or make music.

• Wind down before bedtime. If you take papers home with you and work up to the last minute, you may take your work into disturbed sleep.

• The strategies will be different for each woman, and it helps to share ideas with others who are facing the same challenges, so find, or start up, a working mothers group.

Weaning

One way of thinking about weaning is that it is a matter of introducing cow's milk (or formula milk) and solid foods to a baby's diet in place of breastmilk. That is, it is taking something away from the baby. Another approach is to think of weaning as adding solid foods with perhaps some formula milk as well, but not taking away the breastmilk. The advantage of this second approach is that the baby receives additional nutrition, rather than supplementary foods. Without doubt, the best food for a baby throughout the first year is breastmilk. Milk in one form or another should form the major part of a baby's diet well into the second year of life.

Solid foods can be added in very small tastes as soon as the baby is interested in them, but there is no nutritional benefit in offering them until the baby is six months old. If you decide to offer foods in addition to, rather than in place of, breastmilk, do so *after* breastfeeds, not before.

WEANING FOODS

A baby needs mushy foods to begin with, though they may seem too soft and bland to you. He has to be able either to roll the food into a ball with his tongue or to slurp it down. He obviously cannot chew yet.

Start your baby on a rice cereal, rather than wheat, as some babies cannot tolerate wheat. Make the cereal with expressed breastmilk rather than artificial or cow's milk, to avoid any possible allergic reaction. Be careful not to overfeed your baby with cereal or he will have no appetite for milk. This quickly leads to a reduction in your output.

Fresh vegetables and fruit purées are other good first foods. Be aware, however, that beets turn the stools red, as though they had blood in them. If you do not scrape away the stringy parts of banana, the stools sometimes look as if they contain threadworms. Any food that is not completely digested may produce lumpy stools. If you want to start a baby on meat dishes, be sure the fat content is low.

Slices of apple and banana and other finger foods are fun to eat. A baby explores new tastes and textures and experiments with careful finger movements.

When babies start teething, they enjoy zwieback. Rice crackers are good for the baby who cannot tolerate wheat. Babies like food they can gnaw, carrots and apples, for example. But never leave a baby unattended with food like this, in case a piece catches in his throat.

FOODS TO AVOID

Offer your baby only a couple of teaspoons of each new food to begin with, and try out one food at a time. Wait several days before introducing another, so that you can observe the effect of each. This is important if there are allergies in your or your partner's families. The first sign of an allergy or food intolerance is often a runny nose. You may think your baby has caught a cold. There may be no rash. Recurrent ear infections, dry skin, or an angry-looking red rash may develop later. Eczema appears on the eyebrows and scalp, and behind the ears, and on other parts of the body—the skin creases behind the knees and elbows, for example.

Never persuade a child to "take one more spoonful for Mommy," or force a food. There may be a good reason why he is refusing it. Foods most likely to cause allergic reactions are cow's milk, eggs, citrus fruits, strawberries nuts (many vegetable oils include nut oils), fish, beef, soya, and tomatoes. Keep a diary of foods you introduce and, if you suspect one, return to the simplest first foods that you know your baby can tolerate. Many babies want breastmilk only during the most acute phase of food intolerance. Though medical tests can be done, your own observation is the best way of solving the problem.

The first solid foods should contain no added sugar, or very little, and no salt. Honey is a form of sugar. Sucrose, glucose, fructose, and dextrose are all sugar by other names. Bottled fruit drinks contain glucose and fructose. If you choose baby foods in cans or jars, check the nutritional information on the labels first. It is often difficult to interpret what they really contain. "Low sugar" means almost anything, and sometimes "no added sugar" appears on foods in which no one would think of putting sugar anyway. Avoid soft cheese, chocolate, and foods containing artificial additives. High-fiber foods are not good for babies, either. They fill their stomachs with bulk without providing enough calories for energy and growth.

INTRODUCING COW'S MILK

When you start giving your baby ordinary cow's milk it should be whole milk, because the vital fat-soluble vitamins A and D are in the cream. Until the baby is into the second year of life cow's milk should be boiled.

It may be better for someone other than you to offer a bottle, since the baby expects you to give the breast. It can be difficult to get a baby to take a bottle after the first three months. You can use a spoon and cup, or a special mug, and continue to breastfeed at other times.

HOW LONG TO BREASTFEED?

Breastfeed for as long as you and the child are happy with it. In many societies children thrive when breastfed for three years or more. They are given other foods as well, of course. In China children sometimes go to school with mother's milk in their thermos flasks!

Some toddlers continue to have a feed in the middle of the night when they are no longer having daytime feeds simply because it is easier to feed a child than to explain that he cannot have the breast. Your partner may have to take over at night and offer water.

The feed before going to bed is often the last one to be dropped because it helps the child feel secure and relaxed before sleep. You can gradually reduce the length of this feed and introduce other comfort rituals (see page 153).

THE EFFECT ON YOUR BREASTS

As you reduce the number, frequency, and length of feeds, you produce less milk, though some women find milk in their breasts as long as a year after weaning. Sudden weaning is likely to cause engorgement or milk stasis. Your breasts will return to their prepregnancy size, but will be rather more pendulous—a result of pregnancy rather than breastfeeding.

Arrange for your child to eat with other children who are enjoying solid foods. It is much more fun eating with friends than eating alone.

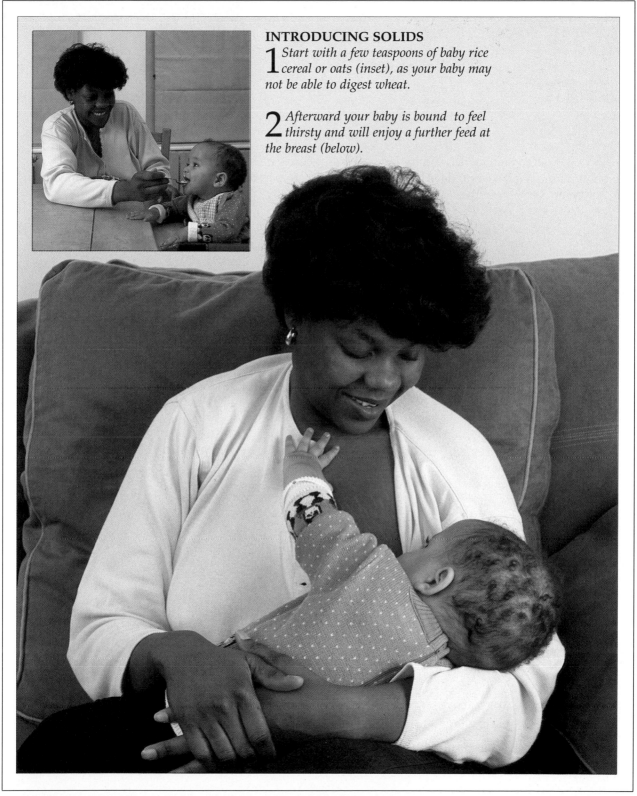

INTRODUCING SOLIDS

1 *Start with a few teaspoons of baby rice cereal or oats (inset), as your baby may not be able to digest wheat.*

2 *Afterward your baby is bound to feel thirsty and will enjoy a further feed at the breast (below).*

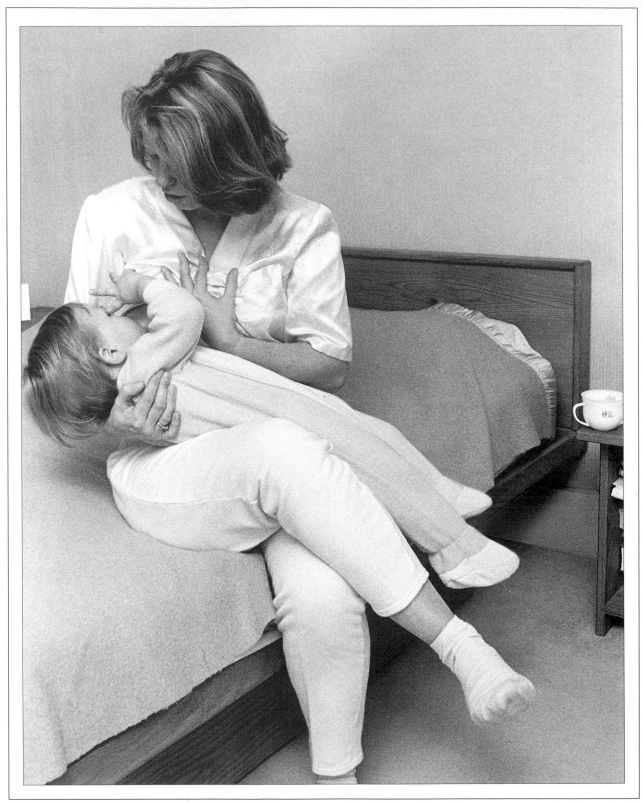

ENDING NIGHTTIME FEEDS

1 *To wean a child off a bedtime breastfeed (opposite), make this feed short, then introduce other comfort rituals, such as offering a drink in a special cup and having a cuddle.*

2 *If you are trying to cut out a breastfeed at night, it is best if your partner attends to the baby when he wakes. If you go to him, he will expect the breast.*

3 *Your partner can offer a drink of water in a bottle (below)—not juice, as this causes tooth decay—and have a special cuddle. Gradually the child will learn not to expect the breast.*

4 *After a few comforting words giving reassurance and security, and another goodnight kiss (below right), tuck the child up in bed again. Be patient—it may take a little while before the child stops waking up in the night expecting a feed.*

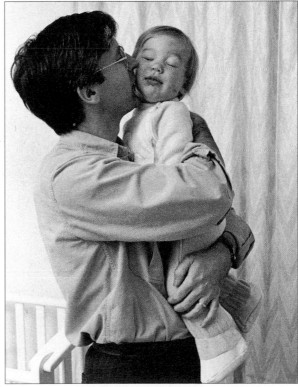

Eating can be a pleasurable social occasion. This is especially important if you are concerned that your child does not have much of an appetite or eats a limited range of foods.

SOLVING PROBLEMS

"Help! What Can I Do?"

THINKING AHEAD

Ten years ago I had an operation to reduce the size of my breasts. Will I be able to breastfeed?
It depends on how much glandular tissue the surgeon removed and whether your nipples were re-sited. In one study, only two of twenty-two women who had aesthetic mammary operations were unable to breastfeed because they could not produce milk. There is every chance that you will breastfeed successfully.*

My baby is due any day now. One of my nipples is flat and the other is inverted. When a nurse looked at them, she warned me that I may not be able to breastfeed.
Offer the breast to your baby as soon as possible after the birth, before your breasts swell with milk, as it is easier for the baby to latch on then. Most babies latch on, with a little help, even when nipples do not protrude at all. Babies suckle at the breast, not the nipple. Once you manage to get the baby well latched, she will gradually mold your nipple into a good shape by sucking on the breast. If you are engorged, manually express or pump some milk before putting the baby to the breast (see page 136).

You can stimulate your nipples by gently rolling them between your thumb and index finger. Just stroking them may make them pop out. Your partner can help by kissing them, too! If you do not have a partner, or don't like this idea, a little crushed ice held against the nipple before you offer the baby the breast may make the nipple more pronounced (see pages 14–16).

Avoid using your finger and thumb to pinch the nipple as you offer the breast. Sometimes this is recommended but it doesn't work, and often only presses the nipple in farther. Instead, rest your thumb lightly on the breast about a finger's length above the nipple, and cup your fingers underneath your breast, both to support it and to enable the baby to target the nipple right on so she can get a good latch.

Holding the baby with her legs under your arm will allow you to get control over the maneuvre. Sometimes it's called "the football hold," but I prefer to call it "the French loaf hold." It's as if you were holding three or four French loaves under your arm with your hand cupped under the ends protruding in front (see page 26–27). Your baby may take some time to learn to suckle well. Take short breaks and ask someone else to hold the baby if you are both becoming frantic. While you breathe out, drop your shoulders and relax so that you are calm and confident before you start again. Never force a distressed baby onto the breast. This will make you both miserable and make feeding more difficult.*

I have had a partial mastectomy, followed by radiotherapy. Now I am pregnant and want to know if there is any chance of being able to breastfeed.
Before the birth it would be wise to get in touch with a breastfeeding counselor (see page 164). Mastectomy and radiotherapy destroy the milk ducts in the affected breast, but there is no reason why the breast on the other side should not make milk. A woman who overcame initial difficulties with breastfeeding told me, "Using the breast that was left for what it was designed for was incredibly healing."

I have insulin-dependant diabetes. Will I be able to breastfeed?
Yes, but your insulin levels and your diet need careful monitoring. The baby of a diabetic mother is less likely to become diabetic if breastfed, so breastfeeding will benefit the baby. Immediately after the birth your insulin level will drop. Over the next few days your baby's

blood sugar should be measured. He will have received a great deal of glucose from your bloodstream while inside you, and now will have to cope with a sudden drop. Because of this, your baby may be given supplementary glucose by bottle or via an intravenous drip.

Keep in close contact with your diabetes specialist during the months of breastfeeding and when you wean the baby. A diabetic mother is vulnerable to a yeast infection, so look out for this and get it treated quickly.

EARLY DAYS

I've just had an emergency cesarean section and someone has said it will be difficult to breastfeed because the milk may not come in. This is not true. There will be milk for your baby, but it may be tricky at first to find a comfortable position for breastfeeding. For the first few days you may need help positioning the baby. Ask your midwife or your partner to help get the baby well latched on. Keep your baby with you at all times and see if you can arrange for your partner or a close friend to have a bed in your room. If you take whatever drugs for pain relief are offered after a feed, very little medication will get through to the baby (see pages 68–71). See if you can get comfortable lying on your side (see right), perhaps with a pillow behind your back and another under your upper bent leg. If you sit up, place one or two pillows on your lap and put your baby on the pillow to feed him so that you don't lean forward. Or have the baby facing you with his legs under your arm, supporting his shoulder and head with your hand, in the "French loaf hold," still keeping him on a pillow (see pages 26–27).

My two-day-old baby is sleepy all the time and doesn't wake for feeds. I had a long and difficult birth that ended in a vacuum extraction. This is normal after a tiring birth. Your baby may need a rest—and you do too, probably. It may also happen because drugs for pain relief, including tranquilizers, are in the baby's bloodstream. Babies who have been exposed to Demerol are less eager to suck, and may not suck vigorously.*

Women are often told that an epidural does not affect the baby. This is not true. Drugs used in epidurals enter the mother's bloodstream and cross the placenta and can be measured in umbilical cord blood. These drugs can have neurobehavioral effects on the baby, who may then need more time to learn to breastfeed.*

Sometimes hospitals are rather warm, too. Lift and unwrap your baby about three hours after the last feed and talk to her and stimulate her by massaging her using a little lavender essential oil in a carrier oil. In fact, you could keep your baby naked except for a diaper, and cuddle her between your breasts and against your bare skin. Later on, when you are up and about, you can try nestling the baby in a sling, with your bra undone.

If your baby becomes tired during a feed and stops sucking, encourage her to take more by massaging your breast so that milk is gently pressed into her mouth. But remember that a newborn baby's stomach is only the size of a golf ball and a short feed may be quite enough for her at this stage.

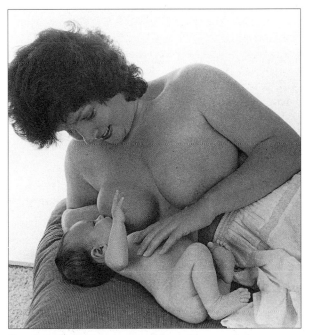

Semi-reclining on your side, with your baby on a firm cushion, protects a cesarean scar from being kicked or pressed on by the baby.

My baby was born three days ago, at 28 weeks, and is in the special-care nursery. I have said I want to breastfeed and have been expressing milk for him to be given by tube. How can I get him off to a good start?
Breastmilk is the ideal food for a premature baby and will help protect him from infection. Tell the nurses that you would prefer him to have breastmilk, unless there are strong reasons for deciding on supplementation. You will need to express milk eight times every 24 hours, including one session during the night, at a time most convenient for you. Express from one breast for five to seven minutes, or until milk is no longer flowing. Then change breasts. After a while you may want to return to the first breast again. This will take about half an hour in all. The milk should be stored in a sterile container. If necessary, it can be refrigerated for up to 24 hours, or frozen.

The "French loaf hold"—the best feeding position if you have had a cesarean or have sore breasts, and it is ideal for premature and other special-care babies.

When you put your baby to the breast, use the "French loaf hold" (see page 26 and below left). Be patient, and coax him to feed by expressing a little colostrum or milk into his mouth and stroking the side of his mouth. At the end of each breastfeed, build up your supply by expressing more milk, that you can store in the refrigerator or the freezer (see pages 136–39).*

My baby has jaundice. I have been told to give her water and that if her bilirubin level does not drop soon I may have to stop breastfeeding.
Bilirubin is a yellow coloring in blood. Large amounts make the skin and the whites of the eyes yellow. It is made by the baby's red blood cells, passes through the liver, and leaves the baby's body via the bowel. Most jaundice is normal and is called "physiological" jaundice (see page 101). Around four out of every ten babies get jaundice on the second or third day and by the end of the first week it has disappeared. This is because during pregnancy your body processes bilirubin for your baby. A few days after the birth, the baby's body learns to do this for itself and the jaundice goes. Raised bilirubin levels in healthy breastfed babies are normal and do not cause damage.*

However, high levels of bilirubin may also occur in the more unusual kinds of jaundice and this can cause brain damage. This is the jaundice pediatricians worry about. It may be the result of blood type incompatibility.

Any baby who has had a difficult birth with subsequent bruising is more vulnerable to jaundice, as are premature and low-birthweight babies. Some drugs used in childbirth also increase the chances of jaundice.

Treatment consists of exposing the baby's whole body to sunlight or, as is usual in hospitals, placing the baby under phototherapy lights or wrapping her in a cocoon of fiber optic light. If a baby has extremely high bilirubin levels, a blood exchange may be given. Put your baby to the breast often—every two or three hours during the day is about right. Her body can deal with the bilirubin more speedily when she gets a lot of breastmilk. Do not leave long intervals between breastfeeds or the jaundice may persist.

If your baby is given phototherapy, ask for it to be done right beside your bed if possible, or stay close to the intensive-care nursery so that you can continue to care for and feed your baby. Take her out from under the lights so that you can cuddle, feed, and talk to her, and remove the blindfold that is used to protect her eyes from the light, so that she can see you.

If you are asked to stop breastfeeding, it will only be for about 48 hours or so, while bilirubin levels are tested. So use a breast pump to stimulate and keep up your milk supply, and freeze your milk for later use (see pages 136–39).

I am terribly engorged. My breasts have blown up like footballs and are hot, hard, and aching. My nipples have almost disappeared. My baby is three days old.

Place hot facecloths on your breasts, shower them with warm water, or kneel in a bath with them hanging down in warm water before the baby comes to the breast. Use a breast pump or hand expression to draw off just enough milk to soften the area around your nipple so that your baby can grasp the breast. Do not pump more than this, or you will step up your production of milk and exacerbate the problem.

With the heel of your palm, gently massage your breast while the baby is sucking. Place ice packs, for example, or a packet of frozen peas or corn wrapped in a cloth, or a plastic bag of crushed ice, against your breasts after a feed (see pages 64–66). Feed your baby every two hours.

Using the "French loaf hold" (see opposite), start on the breast that is most full and let him suck for up to 20 minutes on each breast. If he doesn't want the second breast, hand-express or use a breast pump until you are comfortable.

Wait until your baby drops off the breast at the end of a feed. Don't attempt to pull the baby off. If you need to, insert your pinkie in his mouth to release the suction.

Meanwhile you may need to do something about the pain. If it is bad enough and you need pain relief, take two acetaminophen (Tylenol) about half an hour before the baby is likely to wake for a feed. Then press an ice pack against the sore nipple just before you put your baby to the breast. After he feeds, let your nipples dry in the air. Wear cotton next to your breasts—a cotton bra and a cotton T-shirt, for example—and leave the flaps of your bra open when you feel comfortable doing so. Whenever possible, go topless between feeds. Avoid nipple shields. If you need breast pads to protect your clothing, make sure they do not have plastic backing, and change them as soon as they get soggy.

Nagging doubts

I have read about the milk ejection reflex, but can't feel anything happening. Maybe I'm not making milk.

If you have stitches that are pulling tight after an episiotomy, or have a cesarean section wound, acute discomfort can block your perception of the subtle ways in which your breasts are responding to your baby's need to be fed, and to the feelings as the baby grasps your breast. It does not mean that you have no milk ejection reflex.

Moreover, some women never feel a strong ejection reflex, yet breastfeed successfully. Others experience a reflex and don't like it because it hurts. Still others find it a satisfying feeling. Many do not experience the reflex until breastfeeding is well established—after ten days or so. It is often not until the baby settles down to a steady rhythm of sucking that you become aware of tingling as milk gushes down into the sinuses just behind the nipple. You may have strong uterine contractions as your baby sucks, sometimes called "after pains." These are a sign of the interconnection of breast and uterus. These contractions, which are firming up the uterus into its prepregnancy size and shape, can be uncomfortable and even painful (especially if this is your second or subsequent pregnancy, or if you've had more than one baby this time), but they are a sign that the milk ejection reflex is working (see page 53).

I work out at a local gym. Does exercise affect the milk?

Yes, sometimes, but only if you stretch yourself to the limit; this results in a build up of lactic acid, especially if your diet is high in carbohydrates. Some babies reject milk that is high in lactic acid, as this may alter the taste. Enjoy your workouts, but don't push yourself to a point where you feel stressed. You are the best judge of any effect that the intensity of exercise has on your baby.

BREAST PROBLEMS

I have an inflamed, tender lump in my right breast. What can I do?
The lump is most likely caused by a blocked milk duct. This often occurs in the right breast if you are right-handed and the left breast if you are left-handed, because it is not as easy to position the baby so that she is well latched on with your "wrong" hand. It can happen after you have gone a long time without feeding, and you discover it in the early morning or after the baby has missed a feed. The answer is to breastfeed more often. Each time start with the breast that has the lump—every two hours is about right if your baby is interested. Use the "French loaf hold" (see pages 26–27) on that side so that you help the baby to get a perfect latch. Make sure that your bra is not too tight and that no clothing is pressing on your breast. Vigorous exercise will help, if it is not too painful: wash or polish the floor, clean some windows, or play a game of tennis. Soak a cloth in hot water and place this over the lump or red patch for 15 or 20 minutes before you pick up the baby for a feed. Massage the sore area with your thumb during the feed (see pages 64–66).

If you have a tender red lump and are feverish, too, you may have a breast infection. This is common and, as only a patch of breast tissue is affected and not your milk, you need not give up breastfeeding. In fact, if you stop breastfeeding you are more likely to develop a breast abscess that has to be cut and drained, and this is a very traumatic experience. Treat an infection as you would a blocked duct—which probably caused it in the first place—and if it has not gone away after a couple of days, ask your doctor for antibiotics. Breastfeed as often as you can.

If you have a lump that does not go away after a few weeks, even if it is not painful, see your doctor. It is probably a cyst or benign tumor, and is highly unlikely to be cancer.

My baby has had no problems with feeding, but now, at five weeks, my nipples are sore and itchy. He latches on well. What can I do?
You may have thrush (candida). Look in your baby's mouth and see if there are little white patches on his tongue or cheeks. When a baby develops a yeast infection, it is quickly conveyed to the mother's nipples, which get red, tender, and swollen and often become cracked. The answer is to treat both you and the baby. See your doctor, who will prescribe drops for the baby and a cream for your nipples. The course lasts five or six days. Continue treatment even after the symptoms have disappeared. If it doesn't work in that time, your doctor can prescribe other anticandida drugs.

It will help if you go topless when you can. When dressed, wear a cotton bra, and avoid using breast pads or anything that presses against your nipples.

Express a few drops of milk before bringing the baby to the breast and start him on the side that is less sore, massaging your breast during the feed to encourage free milk flow. Leave your nipples to dry in the air after each feed. If you need pain relief, take acetaminophen about half an hour before the baby is likely to wake for a feed.

Dermatitis is another possible cause of late-onset sore nipples. With dermatitis there is usually a burning feeling, too. It may be an allergic reaction to a cream or spray; as soon as you stop using the product, your nipples will improve.

If you are prone to developing eczema, you may develop it on and around your nipples. Contact your doctor.

UNEXPECTED DIFFICULTIES

I am in bed with the flu. Should I continue to breastfeed? Will my baby catch it?
It is important to go on breastfeeding, as antibodies in your milk will help to protect your baby. Breastfeed as often as you can to keep your milk supply from falling off, and check with a breastfeeding counselor or your doctor to ensure that any drugs you are taking are safe during lactation. Drink plenty of fluids so that you do not get dehydrated. If your baby does get ill, continue to breastfeed—it is the best kind of care you can

give. If she develops an ear infection, sore throat, or stuffy nose and is feverish, get your doctor's advice about treatment. The baby may not be able to breathe, suck, and swallow at the same time, and may be in pain. The doctor can prescribe antibiotic drops and nose drops. You may also find that it helps if you breastfeed with your baby more or less upright.

Your baby is likely to want to feed little and often. Offer her frequent feeds so that she does not become dehydrated (see page 56), and, if you have one, use a humidifier.

I have to go back into the hospital for an operation and will be separated from my fully breastfed baby for 24–36 hours. What can I do?
First, see if the hospital can admit you to a single room where you can have your baby with you all the time, and where your partner or a close friend can have a cot set up and stay with you to help with the baby. This would be by far the best solution. Sometimes arrangements can be made for a nursing mother to be on the maternity ward, where the midwives and nurses will understand your needs, as well as those of the baby.

In any situation where you know that you must be parted from your baby, either manually express or pump milk after each feed before the separation (see pages 136–139). Start this well in advance so that you know that you have a good store of either refrigerated milk, or, if it has to be kept longer than 24 hours, frozen milk. Three such postbreastfeeding expressions should produce one complete bottle-feed of breastmilk. So you can base your arithmetic on that estimate.

Unless you are very confident with manual expression, take an electric pump with you to the hospital so that you do not get engorged and can keep producing milk. If you are in a maternity ward, ask the hospital to let you have a pump. The nurses can store the milk in a refrigerator.

The other possibility if you live near the hospital is that someone may be able to bring your baby to the hospital frequently. Ask the surgeon and the anesthetist what medication you will have to take. There are often alternative drugs that can be used in place of those that are inadvisable during breastfeeding. Usually by the time you have come

around from a general anesthetic, it is safe to breastfeed. If you are prescribed drugs that are unsafe during lactation, you will need to express and throw away the milk produced while you are taking the drugs (see pages 68–71).

IT'S NOT WORKING. . .

My baby son is seven weeks old and is not putting on weight any longer and the doctor thinks I should top up with formula or stop breastfeeding. What can I do to increase my milk supply?
Babies often have growth spurts, starting at about six weeks, when they need extra breastmilk. Set aside one day for the 24-Hour Peak Production Plan (see page 106) to increase your output.

If you possibly can, put a note on your door saying "Mother and Baby Resting," go to bed with the baby for a couple of days and the night between, cuddle and play with him, and feed at every opportunity. During each feed, when his rate of swallowing to sucking slows, change breasts. Then, when the rate of swallowing to sucking slows down on that breast, change back again. By this time the first breast will have made more milk. Go on like this for half an hour, or until your baby drops into a satisfied sleep. There is no point in drinking more than you want, but keep some water or other fluids beside you so that you do not get thirsty. If your baby is still not thriving, you can introduce a bottle after a feed at which he is obviously unsatisfied. You may find this only happens with the early-evening feed.

Avoid test-weighing before and after feeds. It gives very inaccurate readings, is a waste of time, and usually only adds to your natural anxieties about your baby's wellbeing.

My baby starts sucking, then pulls away from my breast and cries. What am I doing wrong?
Thrush, earache, a stuffed-up nose, or sore throat are the most common reasons for a baby's pulling away from the breast. Sometimes the baby will take your expressed milk from a cup and spoon or from a bottle. If necessary, express your milk while you treat the underlying cause and until the baby is comfortable.

A baby sometimes comes to the breast eagerly, latches on, but then pulls back, crying, as if you were offering her poison. These may be early difficulties arising from her inexperience. Be patient and persevere.

Occasionally a baby reacts to something you have eaten that has changed the flavor of your milk, or, perhaps, to which you have some intolerance even though you were unaware of it. Dairy products (especially cow's milk and cheeses), strong coffee or caffeine medications, curry, large quantities of fruit or juices, fish, peanuts, cabbage, onions, pulses, citrus fruits, and tomatoes sometimes do this. You could try cutting out one of these foods, and then introducing it again gradually to observe whether your baby has a reaction to the food. If your baby has a food intolerance, or even a full-fledged allergy, you may still be able to have a small quantity of a food or drink that causes problems only when it is taken in large amounts. The cause is unlikely to be a food intolerance if the baby's stools are normal. But if they are green, or if he has a lot of wind and is obviously irritable, and he doesn't have an infection, it is worth looking at dietary causes.

My two-month-old son spits up milk after every feed. Is there anything I can do about it?
Most babies "posset"—regurgitate some milk after a feed—especially if they are energetic, excitable feeders. Sometimes it seems as if they have spit up most of the milk, but it usually looks like much more than it is.

Projectile vomiting is the kind that shoots out as if from a garden hose. It can happen when a baby is healthy but has simply taken a feed too fast. Sometimes, however, it is caused by pyloric stenosis, a stomach obstruction. If the vomiting gets worse and worse and, especially if the baby loses weight, see your doctor. Surgery may be necessary. Several hours after the operation you will be able to breastfeed again. Breastmilk is easily digested, so breastfeeding is the best way to care for a baby after surgery.

My baby, who is two-and-a-half months old, cries a lot. It started when she was six weeks old, and makes me feel I must be doing everything wrong.
You may have to learn to live with it. Some babies are more expressive than others and cry not only when they are hungry, but when they are overstimulated, understimulated (bored), lonely, or, of course, in pain. This crying often continues until the baby develops other ways of letting you know what she wants, and until she can comfort herself. These skills develop at about four months.

Giving your breast lets your baby know that you care. Even when she is not really hungry, sucking is comforting for her.

If you are producing a lot of milk, your baby may be getting too much foremilk—the sort that is thirst-quenching but unsatisfying. Some babies gulp a great deal of foremilk but never get to the milk that is rich in fat at the end of a feed. This results in lactose building up in the bowels and causing colic. With these babies it may help to offer one breast at each feed, switching to the other only when no more milk is flowing from the first breast. The baby gets a full feed from one breast and a top-up from the other.

Mothers with crying babies often find that reverberating noise helps. Place the baby near the washing machine or clothes dryer, use the vacuum cleaner, or play music—any kind of noise you like. Movement usually helps, too, so try dancing with her to your favorite music. Change her position frequently. Walk holding her in a sling against your body. Rock her. Or take her for a drive in the car.

At night she may be more contented if you have her in your bed, where you can slip her a breast whenever she stirs, before she gets upset. Some babies like being packaged firmly, cocoonlike, or even swaddled. Others hate it. Water is comforting, too. When you can make space for it in your life, bathe her or get into a warm bath with her, perhaps with some music on and candlelight flickering.

You will need a break from the baby to get some exercise or to sleep every day, to avoid becoming distressed and exhausted yourself. It will help if you can find another mother who has a crying baby, as one of the main problems is the isolation and sense of guilt that having a crying baby brings (see pages 120–22).

I am breastfeeding my 16-month-old and am pregnant again. I have considered weaning him, but he enjoys the breast, and it is a time when I can put my feet up and relax.
You can continue to breastfeed during pregnancy, but make sure you have a good diet, with lots of fresh fruit and vegetables and whole-grain foods. Your breasts and nipples may be more tender than usual, a result of the hormonal adjustment to pregnancy. In midpregnancy your milk supply may be diminished, and some children wean themselves when this happens. In the last weeks your milk will change to get ready for the new baby. Some older nursing babies do not like the taste when this happens and wean themselves at this point. But children often nurse enthusiastically again once the baby is born and colostrum has given way to mature milk. You should be able to breastfeed two babies without difficulty, but always put the younger baby to the breast first. When tandem feeding is going well it saves work. It also gives comfort to the older child when it is most needed because there is a new member of the family (see page 116), who everyone is admiring and cooing over.*

FEEDING AN OLDER BABY

My baby is six months old and is putting on weight very slowly. She is breastfed and has three meals a day, too. She has started to sleep through the night. Does this mean I should wean her?
No. She still benefits from your milk, so if you and she enjoy breastfeeding, carry on, offering her the breast before giving solid food. If your milk supply is dwindling, try offering her longer at the breast and make sure that intervals between feeds are no more than four hours. You can step up the supply with the 24-Hour Peak Production Plan (see page 106). If necessary, see if you can arrange to have time off work so that you can do this. If she is sleeping through the night, be sure that you give her a leisurely bedtime feed and a good long cuddle and breastfeed early in the morning. Change breasts when the swallow-to-suck rate slows down, and then change her back to the first breast again, and so on. You will find that she soon starts putting on weight. But don't expect her to conform to some baby weight prediction chart; she is an individual who will put on weight at her own pace (see page 56).

My baby is teething and she has suddenly started biting me, usually toward the end of a feed. I see a wicked gleam in her eye and then she snaps at me. I am worried that she will really hurt me when her teeth come in.
Biting is common during teething, but not so common once the teeth are there. Take her straight off the breast, say "No" firmly, and, depending on her reaction, put her down for a while. Never hit her and never leave her screaming. Instead, be quietly consistent. Give her an ice-cold teething ring to chew on to ease her sore gums.

If she makes you yell, she may think it is a great game, so watch for moments when you realize that she is working up to biting and no longer sucking vigorously. Pop a finger in her mouth, and take her off the breast before she starts biting. Instead, play games that elicit a startle response, like "peek-a-boo." She enjoys getting an excited reaction from you.

USEFUL INFORMATION

If you would like to read more about breastfeeding, there is a book of mine called *The Experience of Breastfeeding*. You can find more about sex and breastfeeding in another of my books, *Woman's Experience of Sex*. Both titles are published by Penguin.

BREASTFEEDING ORGANIZATIONS

La Leche League International (LLLI)
1400 North Meacham Road
P.O. Box 4079
Schaumberg, IL 60168-4079
Tel: 1-800-LA-LECHE or 847-519-7730
Order Dept: 847-519-9585
Fax: 847-519-0035
www.laleche.org
The largest breastfeeding organization in the U.S., with branches in 42 countries. They offer counseling, advice, and referrals. La Leche also sells books and products for breastfeeding. Call the 800 number for your local group and counselor.

International Lactation Consultants Association (ILCA)
4101 Lake Boone Trail
Raleigh, NC 27607
Tel: 919-787-5181 Fax: 919-787-4916
www.ilca.org
Provides referrals to local professional lactation consultants, hosts conferences, and publishes educational material.

National Alliance for Breastfeeding Advocacy (NABA)
245 Conant Road
Weston, MA 02193
Tel: 617-893-3553 Fax: 617-893-8608
The national leadership organization for promoting breastfeeding in the U.S. It sponsors advocacy programs, monitors legislation, and publishes educational papers and newsletters.

OTHER USEFUL ORGANIZATIONS

Human Milk Banking Association of North America (HMBANA)
8 Jan Sebastian Way, # 13
Sandwich, MA 02563
Tel: 888-232-8809 or 508-888-4041
Fax: 508-888-8050

National Downs Syndrome Congress
1605 Chantilly Drive, Suite 250
Atlanta, GA 30324
Tel: 800-232-6372 or 404-633-1555
Fax: 404-633-2817
members.carol.net/ndsc

The Cleft Palate Foundation
1829 East Franklin Street, Suite 1022
Chapel Hill, NC 27514
Tel: 800-24-CLEFT or 919-933-9044
Fax: 919-933-9604
www.cleft.com

Cleft palate nipples are available from:

Medela, Inc. (see below)

Ross Products Division
Shipping Services
2141 Southwest Blvd., Suite L
Grove City, OH 43123-1896
Tel: 800-227-5767 or 614-624-4683

BREAST PUMPS

The following companies sell and lease breast pumps. Most of them also offer other breastfeeding accessories and child care items: call the numbers provided for product catalogs.

Avent America, Inc.
501 Lively Boulevard
Elk Grove Village, IL 60007-2013
Tel: 800-542-8368
Fax: 847-228-6142

Medela, Inc.
P.O. Box 660
McHenry, IL 60051-0660
Tel: 800-435-8316 or 815-363-1166
Fax: 800-995-7867
www.medela.com

White River Concepts
924 C Calle Negocio
San Clemente, CA 92673
Tel: 800-342-3906 or 714-366-8960
Fax: 714-366-1664
www.whiteriver.com

Bosom Buddies, Inc.
1554 Emerson
Denver, CO 80218
Tel: 888-860-0041 or 303-860-0041
Fax: 303-770-1422
www.bosombuddies.com

American Homecare Products (AHC)
11140 Rockville Pike, Suite 101
Rockville, MD 20852
Tel: 888-633-7759 or 301-881-6009
www.4yourback.com

Lactation Innovation
2415 Nottingham
Naperville, IL 60565
Tel: 888-522-8468 or 630-357-0028
www.mcs.net/~talmadge

Knox Breastfeeding Accessories
P.O. Box 187
Mount Vernon, OH 43050-0187
www.spiker.net/betz

Little Koala
614 Bellefonte St.
Shadyside, PA 15232
Tel: 412-687-1239
www.littlekoala.com

Mother Moon
33 Pine Road
North Hampton, NH 03862
Tel: 603-964-7663
www.mothermoon.com

WEB SITES

These are only a few of the most helpful sites. You can find scores of links on your own by starting at these pages, or by using any major search engine.

"The Breastfeeding Advocacy Page"
www.clark.net/pub/activist/bfpage/bfpage.html

"The Breastfeeding Page"
www3.islandnet.com/~bedford/brstfeed.html

"Breastfeeding Links"
users.aol.com/kristachan/bflink.htm

"Femina" www.femina.com

"ParentPlace"
www.parentsplace.com

"Parenttime"
www.parenttime.com

"BabyCenter"
babycenter.com

"Wide Smiles: Cleft Lip and Palate Resource"
www.widesmiles.org

REFERENCES

BIBLIOGRAPHY

• Inch, S., and Fisher, C. "Mastitis: infection or inflammation?" *Practitioner*, 239, pp. 472–76, August 1995.

• Pryor, Gale *Nursing Mother, Working Mother*, Harvard Common Press, Boston, 1997.

• Huggins, Kathleen *The Nursing Mother's Companion*, Harvard Common Press, Boston, 1990.

• Fisher, C. "Translating normal breastfeeding management into the neonatal unit," *CMA Medical Data*, 6,1, p. 80, 1996.

SPECIFIC REFERENCES

The numbers in **bold** refer to the pages on which the reference * appears.

p. 6 Kitzinger, Sheila *Woman's Experience of Sex*, Penguin Books, 1985.

p. 7 Howie, Peter W., Forsyth, J. Stewart, Ogston, Simon A., Clark, Ann, and Florey, Charles du V. "Protective effect of breastfeeding against infection," *British Medical Journal*, 300, pp. 11–16, 1990.
• Bogaard, C., van den. Hogen, H. J. M., van den. Juygen, F. J. A., and Weel, C van. "The relationship between breastfeeding and early childhood morbidity in a general population," *Family Medicine*, 23, pp. 510–15, 1991.
• Editorial "The warm chain for breastfeeding," *Lancet*, 344: pp. 1239-40, 1994.

p. 18 Newton, Niles "The hormone of love," paper given at Ninth International Congress of Psychosomatic Obstetrics & Gynaecology, Amsterdam, 1989.

p. 46 Schal, B. Montagner, H. Hertling, E. et al. "Les stimulations olfactives dans les rèlations entre l'enfant et la mère," *Reprod Nutr Dev*, 20, pp. 843–858, 1980.
• Righard L. Alade MO. "Effect of delivery room routines on success of first breastfeed," *Lancet*, 336: pp. 1105–1107, 1990.

p. 62 Sharp, Donald "Moist wound healing for sore or cracked nipples," *Breastfeeding Abstracts*, 12, 2, p. 1, 1992.

• Hale, Thomas W. *Medications and Mothers' Milk*, Sixth Edition, p. 598, Amarillo, Texas, 1997.
• Hansen, T. W. R. "Nipple vasospasm in the breastfeeding woman," *Clinical Pediatrics*, 35, pp. 309–31, 6 June 1996.

p. 65 Inch, S., and Fisher, C. *Practitioner*, op. cit.

p. 68 Wilkin, T. J. "Early Nutrition and Diabetes Mellitus," *British Medical Journal*, 306, no. 6873, pp. 283–84, 1993.
• Hale, Thomas W. *Medication and Mothers' Milk*, op.cit.
• Yoshida, K. and Kumar, R. "Breastfeeding and psychotropic drugs," *International Review of Psychiatry*, 8, pp. 117–24, 1996.
• Yoshida, K., Smith, B., Craggs, M. and Kumar, R. "Neuroleptic drugs in breastmilk: a study of pharmacokinetics and of possible effects in breastfed infants," *Psychological Medicine*, 28, pp. 81–91, 1998.

p. 69 Hale, Thomas W. *Medication and Mothers' Milk*, op.cit.

p. 78 "Infant Feeding 1995," Office for National Statistics, London: HM Stationary Office, 1997.
• Walker, Marsha "Do Labor Medications Affect Breastfeeding?" *Journal of Human Lactation*, 13, 2, pp. 131–37, June 1997.
• Walker, Marsha "Breastfeeding the Sleepy Baby," *Journal of Human Lactation*, 13, 2, pp. 151–53, June 1997.

p. 98 Lucas, A., and Cole, T. J. "Breastmilk and neonatal necrotising enterocolitis," *Lancet*, 336, pp. 1519–23, Dec 22–29 1990.

p. 101 Nicoll, A. et al. "Supplementary feeding and jaundice in newborns," *Acta Paediatrica Scandinavica*, 71, 5, pp. 759–61, 1982.
• de Carvalho, M. et al. "Effects of water supplementation on jaundice in breastfed infants," *Archives of Diseases of Childhood*, 56, 7, pp. 568–69, 1981.

p. 104 Winnicott, D. W. "Babies and their Mothers," Addison-Wesley, Reading, Massachusetts, p.31, 1987.

p. 134 Franklin, A. L. et al. "Breastfeeding and respiratory virus infection," *Pediatrics*, 70, pp. 239–45, 1982.

p. 138 Esterik, Penny van. "Expressing Ourselves: Breast Pumps," *Journal of Human Lactation*, 12, 4, p. 273, 1996.

p. 140 Kitzinger, Jenny "Recalling the Pain," *Nursing Times*, 86, 3, 1990.

p. 146 National Institute of Child Health and Development 1997.

p. 147 Howie, Peter W. et al. "Protective effect of breastfeeding against infection," *British Medical Journal*, op. cit.

p. 156 Deutinger, M., and Deutinger, J. *Surgery, Gynecology and Obstetrics*, 176, 3, pp. 267–70, March 1993.
• Alexander, Jo M., Grant, Adrian M., Campbell, Michael J. "Randomised controlled trial of breast shells and Hoffman's exercises for inverted and non-protractile nipples," *British Journal of Midwifery*, 304, 6833, 18 April 1992.

p. 157 Nissen, E., Lilja, G., Matthiesen, A. S. et al. *Acta Paediatrica*, 84, 2, pp. 140–45, February 1995.
• Walker, Marsha "Do Labor Medications Affect Breastfeeding?" *Journal of Human Lactation*, op. cit.
• Walker, Marsha "Breastfeeding the Sleepy Baby," op. cit.

p. 158 Ingram J., Redshaw, M., Harris A. "Breastfeeding in neonatal care," *British Journal of Midwifery*, 2, 9, pp. 412–18, September 1994.
• Newman, T. B., and Maisels, M. J. "Does hyper bilirubinemia damage the brain of healthy full-term infants?" *Clinics in Perinatology*, 17, pp. 331–58, 1990.
• McDonagh, A. F. "Is bilirubin good for you?" *Clinics in Perinatology*, 17, pp. 359–60, 1990.
• Martinez, Jose C., Rea, Martina, and de Zoysa, Isabelle, "Breast feeding in the first six months," *BMJ* 304, 6834, pp. 1068-1069, 1992.

p. 163 Moscone, S. R., Moore, M. J. "Breastfeeding during pregnancy," *Journal of Human Lactation*, 9, 2, pp. 83–88, June 1993.

INDEX

ACKNOWLEDGMENTS

The author would like to thank Chloe Fisher and Sally Inch of the breastfeeding clinic at the John Ratcliffe Hospital, Oxford, and Channi Kumar, Professor of Perinatal Psychiatry at the Maudsley Hospital, for their helpful advice and expertise.

The publishers would like to thank the following for their help in producing this book:

Index Hilary Bird

DTP work Rajen Shah

Editorial assistance Clair Savage, Anna Scobie

Illustrations Tony Graham

Photographic credits Tom Worsley

News Team International Ltd for the photograph of the author on page 4.
Lennart Neilson, page 9. Medela, page 102. Belinda Whiting, page 103. Egnell Ameda and Medela for the images of breastpumps on page 139.

The publishers would also like to thank all the women and their families who agreed to be photographed.